The International Handbook of Computer Security

Jae K. Shim, Ph.D.
Anique A. Qureshi, Ph.D., CPA, CIA
Joel G. Siegel, Ph.D., CPA

Glenlake Publishing Company, Ltd.
Chicago • London • New Delhi

Fitzroy Dearborn Publishers
Chicago and London

GPCo
1261 West Glenlake
Chicago, IL 60660
glenlake@ix.netcom.com

Dedication

Chung Shim
Dedicated Wife

Shaheen Qureshi
Loving Wife

Aqsa Qureshi
Wonderful Daughter

Roberta Siegel
Loving Wife, Colleague, and Partner

Acknowledgements

We express our deep appreciation to Barbara Evans for her exceptional editing efforts. Special thanks go to Jimmy Chang, microcomputer consultant at Rand Corporation in Santa Monica for coauthoring Chapters 3 and 4, to Allison Shim for her word processing work, and to Roberta Siegel for contributing her expertise in computer security.

We acknowledge with great appreciation the advice and suggestions of Dr. John Walker, CPA, an internationally recognized leading expert on computer security.

Table of Contents

About the Authors

Jae K. Shim, Ph.D., is professor of business administration at California State University, Long Beach. Dr. Shim received his MBA and Ph.D. degrees from the University of California at Berkeley. For over 20 years a consultant on information systems development and computer applications, he is now president of the National Business Review Foundation, a management and computer consulting firm. Dr. Shim has more than 50 books to his credit and has published some 50 articles in professional journals, including the *Journal of Systems Management, Financial Management*, the *Journal of Operational Research, Omega, Data Management, Management Accounting, Simulation and Games, Long Range Planning*, the *Journal of Business Forecasting, Decision Sciences, Management Science*, and *Econometrica*.

In 1982 Dr. Shim received the Credit Research Foundation Outstanding Paper Award for one of his articles on financial modeling. He has also received a Ford Foundation Award, a Mellon Research Fellowship, and an Arthur Andersen Research Grant.

Anique Qureshi, Ph.D., CPA, CIA, is associate professor of accounting and information systems at Queens College of the City University of New York. He is an expert in computer applications, especially those related to the World Wide Web. Dr. Qureshi has written two books for Prentice-Hall and has contributed chapters to books published by both Prentice-Hall and McGraw-Hill. His articles have appeared in *Accounting Technology*, the *CPA Journal, Management Accounting*, the *National Public Accountant*, and *Internal Auditing*.

Joel G. Siegel, Ph.D., CPA, is a consultant to businesses on computer applications and professor of accounting, finance, and information systems, Queens College of the City University of New York. He was previously associated with Coopers and Lybrand, CPAs, and Arthur Andersen,

CPAs. He has served as consultant to numerous organizations including Citicorp, ITT, and the American Institute of Certified Public Accountants (AICPA). Dr. Siegel is the author of 60 books, published by Glenlake Publishing, the American Management Association, Prentice-Hall, Richard Irwin, McGraw-Hill, HarperCollins, John Wiley, Macmillan, Probus, International Publishing, Barron's, and AICPA. He has written over 200 articles on business topics, many on computer applications to business. His articles have appeared in such journals as *Computers in Accounting, Financial Executive, Financial Analysis Journal,* the *CPA Journal, National Public Accountant,* and *Practical Accountant.* In 1972, he received the Outstanding Educator of America Award. Dr. Siegel is listed in Who's Who Among Writers and Who's Who in the World. He formerly chaired the National Oversight Board.

What This Book Will do For You

Computers are an integral part of everyday operations. Organizations depend on them. A computer system failure will have a critical impact on the organization. Potential vulnerabilities in a computer system that could undermine operations must therefore be minimized or eliminated.

The International Handbook of Computer Security is written primarily to help business executives and information systems/computer professionals protect their computers and data from a wide variety of threats. It is intended to provide practical and thorough guidance on a wide range of computer security issues, emphasizing practical guidance rather than theory. Topics discussed include company security policies, physical security, data preservation, hardware and software security, personnel security, network security, contingency planning, and legal and auditing issues.

Security concerns have heightened in recent years. You've probably seen news stories about computer data errors, thefts, burglaries, fires, and sabotage. Moreover, the increased use of networked computers, including the Internet, Intranets, and Extranets, has had a profound effect on computer security. The greatest advantage of remote access through networks—convenience—is what makes the system more vulnerable to loss. As the number of points from which a computer can be accessed increases, so does the threat of attack.

The major steps in managing computer security are discussed in this book. We help you as a business executive identify resources in your own organization that need to be protected. Sometimes, thinking information is not valuable to anyone else, your organization may not be willing to take security precautions.

This is a serious mistake. Hackers often steal or destroy private or confidential data simply because it's there! Other hackers may delete or destroy files in an attempt to cover their illegal activity. You need a comprehensive security plan in your organization; a casual attitude towards computer security is never justified.

We also analyze the costs and benefits of various security safeguards. Cost includes not only the direct cost of a safeguard, such as equipment and installation costs, but also the indirect costs, such as employee morale and productivity losses.

It's important to recognize that increasing security typically results in reduced convenience. Employees may resent the inconvenience that accompanies security safeguards. And indeed, too much security can be just as detrimental as too little. You'll need to find a balance.

We cannot over-emphasize the importance of contingency planning. If security is violated, how do you recover? What are the legal consequences? What will be the financial impact? In planning computer security policies and financial support, be sure to perform a risk analysis.

Computer security risks fall into three major categories: destruction, modification, and disclosure. Each may be further classified into intentional, unintentional, and environmental attacks. One threat comes from computer criminals and disgruntled employees who intend to defraud, sabotage, and "hack." Another comes from computer users who are careless. A final threat comes from the environment; your organization must protect itself from disasters like fire, flood, and earthquakes. An effective security plan must consider all these types of threats.

We do not neglect insurance. What is the company's risk exposure? Your insurance policies should cover such risks as theft, fraud, intentional destruction, and forgery, as well as business interruption insurance to cover additional expenses and lost profits during downtime.

Throughout this book, we provide extensive examples to illustrate practical applications, and answers to common questions. Checklists, charts, graphs, diagrams, report forms, schedules, tables, exhibits, illustrations, and step-by-step instructions are designed to enhance the handbook's practical use. The techniques we spell out can be adopted outright or modified to suit your own needs.

Chapter 1
Organizational Policy

Today the cost to businesses of stolen, misused, or altered information can be high, especially if real or purported damages to customers can be traced back to mismanagement. That's why you must value your information resources within the context of your business goals and constraints.

The objective of security management is to eliminate or minimize computer vulnerability to destruction, modification, or disclosure. But before we can discuss information security, we must see how that security works.

A key consideration is the physical location of the organization. Naturally, more security is needed in areas of high crime, although this may take the form of less expensive generic physical security measures. Who uses the information will also affect the security measures chosen. Some users need to alter data; others simply need to access it.

If a security plan is to be effective, top management must be fully convinced of the need to take counteractive steps. To assess the seriousness of a computer breakdown or loss of data, each business has to evaluate threats to the company, the potential losses if the threats are realized, and the time and cost that will be necessary to recover from any breach in security.

The proliferation of networks scatters security issues across the globe and increases the need for inexpensive but effective levels of security. Physical security measures reflect the location of each component, but procedural measures, especially in a large organization, though they may seem obtrusive are of equal importance.

Personal computers are another potential security threat. More and more people operate their PCs with telecommunications services to connect to central computers and network services. To limit the damage that can be done, each user must be identified and that identity authenticated. The user is then allowed to perform only authorized actions.

Audits can be very valuable for detecting security violations and deterring future violations. A security violation may be indicated from customer or vendor complaints that show discrepancies or errors; on the other hand, variance allowances can cover up fraudulent activity.

Audit trails used to produce exception reports are especially valuable to managers. Standard questions include who accessed what data, whether the data were altered, or whether access-only employees attempted alteration. Exception reports are best used daily because they are after-the-fact reports. You may also choose to look only at reports from areas of high vulnerability or where there is a history of corruption or attempted corruption.

A good manager will know the types and forms of information generated and how the information is used by the business before planning how to manage it. Security measures in an information resource management program must be practical, flexible, and in tune with the needs of the business. A risk-management approach recognizes alternatives and decision choices at each step in information resources management in order to develop a program that meshes with ongoing business practices.

It is your responsibility as a manager to (1) assist with the design and implementation of security procedures and controls, and (2) ensure that these remain effective by continuous internal audits. To do this you must:

- Identify the risks.
- Evaluate the risks.
- Install appropriate controls.
- Prepare a contingency plan.
- Continually monitor those controls against the plan.

Misuse of information is costly. Ask yourself, "Where in the business scheme does this information work?" identifying not only the department but also the type of usage (strategic, tactical, operational, or historical). This will help you determine how secure that information must be. Its value must justify the expense of protecting business data. For instance, because encryption is relatively expensive, it's usually reserved for higher business use (strategic or tactical). Operational business uses may use simpler controls such as passwords.

Security Administration

Security should be administered in the context of how the organization needs to control, use, and protect its information. Protection needs to be appropriate and reasonable given management's risk posture. Three levels of security (physical, procedural, and logical) used in tandem can reduce the risks.

Physical Security

Physical security, the first line of defense, is the one that usually comes to mind when you hear the word "security." This level literally separates those who are authorized to use certain types of information from those who are not. It also creates and maintains an environment in which the equipment is not exposed to damaging environment hazards like extreme heat or flooding, natural disasters, fire, power failure, or air conditioning failure.

Detection devices warn of an environmental failure, and automatic systems can protect against damages. Heat and smoke sensors and thermostats for temperature and humidity are standard equipment in computer centers. Attached to automatic shutoff devices they protect your computer system should critical limits be exceeded. Some natural disasters cannot be foreseen, especially in the usually windowless domain of the computer center, but disruption of service can be kept to a minimum by using backup centers.

At backup centers themselves, physical security takes on a heightened purpose. Your company may want to join a data center insurance group. The group data center should be able to handle the total workload of each member organization; in the event of service failure, the data center assumes the data processing role for that organization. During regular operations the data center may be used by a third party.

Human control is more elusive. Traffic, especially at the beginning and end of the business day, can overburden card-access systems. The physical layout of the building and the routes employees use to reach their workplaces can also overburden checkpoints. Guards, usually low-paid, are susceptible to bribery and relaxation of standards. Additionally, during high traffic times there may not be enough guards to check employee ID badges, or register visitors.

Procedural Security

Daily users of information systems gain great insight into their workings. They can identify holes in the process. Employees generally know if their system is being audited (as they should, to discourage corruption); if they are not being audited, the temptation to tamper with the system may be too great to resist. Companies with high turnover are particularly susceptible to employee modifications of the system.

Careful hiring and processing of employees, then, is one way to instill procedural security. Threats from mentally unstable employees are obvious. However, without the proper safeguards all current and former employees have access to the company's computer resources. Among the proper safeguards:

- Revoke passwords as soon as an employee is terminated or if he is even suspected of infringement.
- Use lists of authorized personnel to control entrance into the system.
- Constantly monitor logs generated by computer systems that report access to sensitive areas.
- All transactions processed should be reviewed and audited.

These actions constitute a fundamental level of control over business operations that lets the whole organization know that management is concerned with security and is devoting time and money to seeing that its security objectives are met.

Logical Security

Computer hardware or software should automatically control the people and programs trying to access computer resources. Data encryption is an example.

Generally, all three levels of security must be combined to form the right mix for a given element. This is called an access control system. Its goals are to:

- Prevent unauthorized physical or logical access to facilities or to information via electronic formats,
- Track user computing and telecommunication activities, and
- Establish a basis for, and then enforce, a set of authorizations for all persons and programs attempting to use electronic information resources.

Establishing a Security Policy

Every organization should have a security policy that defines the limits of acceptable behavior and how the organization will respond to violations of such behavior. The policy assigns accountability and delegates authority across the organization. It will naturally differ from organization to organization, based on unique needs. Optional policies include:

- No playing of computer games on corporate computers.
- No visiting adult web sites using corporate Internet accounts or computers.
- An embargo against the use of a specific protocol if it cannot be administered securely.
- A prohibition against taking copies of certain corporate electronic documents out of the office.
- No use of pirated software.

Questions you must answer include: How will violators be reprimanded or punished? Will the organization respond to violators inside the organization? Will it be different from the response to violators outside the organization? What civil or criminal actions might be taken against violators?

Security policy should not be set piecemeal. This leads to inefficiencies, holes in the system, poor valuation of information elements, and inconsistencies. And it costs more to set policy piecemeal.

Publishing the policy is vital.

The owners of information can best assign information elements to a particular classification. Top management is in the best position to evaluate consequences. About 1 percent of all business information should have the highest level (and therefore costliest) classification. Mid-range classifications typically have about 40 percent of all business information.

Policy statements set program goals, give detailed directions for carrying out procedures, and explain absolute requirements of the information security system. Policy statements should be concise and not require modification for at least five years; standards or procedures usually must be modified no more often than every three years.

Your security policy should be a broad statement that guides individuals and departments as they work to achieve certain goals. Specific actions needed to realize goals will be contained in supporting standards rather than in the policy document.

The security policy should be concise and to the point, generally not exceeding 10 pages. It should be easy to understand. It should emphasize the roles of individuals and departments. It is not the purpose of the security policy to educate individuals. That objective is better achieved through training.

The rationale for a security policy should be stated, explaining its purpose, including why data integrity must be maintained. Come down hard on the importance of maintaining the confidentiality and privacy of information resources. The organization must have information continuously available; any interruption can have serious financial consequences.

Computer security must be everyone's responsibility, so the computer security policy should encompass all locations of the company and all of its subsidiaries. Because security is only as strong as its weakest link, everyone in the organization must be held to the same set of standards. This means that the standards have to be flexible enough to be used in a wide variety of circumstances while remaining consistent across the organization.

The security policies apply to all data and computer facilities, including standalone computers, Internet and Intranet sites, local area networks (LANs), and wide area networks (WANs), as well as all forms of electronic communication, including email, fax, and data transmissions. They should also encompass relevant printed material, such as documentation and technical specifications.

Computer security is a means to an end, not an end in itself; it is an integral component of your organization's overall risk management strategy. It should therefore be evaluated periodically to respond to changes in technology or circumstances. Assign authority for issuing and amending the security policy to a committee such as the Information Technology Management Committee that must determine when circumstances justify departure from the policy. All exceptions must have committee approval.

For a security policy to proceed, all individuals and departments must participate. It is well established that individuals are more likely to accept the security policy (or any other policy!) if they have had input during its creation, but the real benefit of employee participation is the knowledge they bring.

The relationship between the computer security policy and other corporate policies should be spelled out. For example, the computer security policy should be used in conjunction with the firm's policies for the internal control structure and contingency plans, including business interruption and resumption plans.

The policy should ensure compliance with all laws. Privacy and confidentiality issues have a serious effect on computer security. Increased governmental regulation is likely. The legal department should help department heads comply with the laws.

The responsibilities of the Information Systems department and its security personnel should be defined in the security policy document. These responsibilities might be to:

- Be responsible for all computer networks and communications.
- Provide systems development methodology for security needs.
- Ensure that security personnel have the training and skills to perform their duties.
- Provide computer security assistance to other departments.
- Be responsible for all cryptographic methods and keys.
- Manage virus detection software for both networked and stand-alone computers.
- Acquire hardware or operating systems as needed.
- Authorize the use of networks.
- Review, evaluate, and approve all contracts related to information systems.

For personal computer systems, the security policy should address additional precautions; for instance:

- All original data should be backed up regularly.
- Virus detection software must always be used on PCs, especially before copying data or programs onto the network.
- Certain types of confidential or important data should never be stored on a local hard drive; instead such data should be stored on the network, or on floppy or compact disks or a removable hard drive, so that it may be stored in a secure place.
- Standards should be established for remote access.
- PCs should not be directly connected to the Internet, since the Internet is a source of both virus infections and hackers. Internet access should be only through the company's Internet server, which can protect itself.

Additional policy components can include the policies regarding the hiring, performance, and firing of information workers, though they should not be overly specific.

Security should be continuous in all situations, and not limited to protecting against intentional attacks. The board of directors should write a clear statement of security intention, including:

- Definitions of behaviors that will be tolerated or that will result in disciplinary action or dismissal,
- Standards of protection necessary at every company location, and
- Allocation of responsibility to one person (ideally) or to a group, with the authority to carry out the policy, set budgets, and approve objectives.

The Security Administrator

The security administrator sets policy, subject to board approval. He also investigates, monitors, advises employees, counsels management, and acts as a technical specialist.

The security administrator establishes the minimal fixed requirements for information classification and the protection each classification needs in terms of physical, procedural, and logical security elements. He assigns responsibilities to job classifications and explains how to manage exceptions to policy.

The security administrator advises other information security administrators and users on the selection and application of security measures, giving advice on how to mark (written and electronic "stamps") and handle processes, select software security packages, train security coordinators, and solve problems.

The security administrator investigates all computer security violations, advises senior management on matters of information resource control, consults on matters of information security, and provides technical consultation for business activities.

Finally . . .

Finding and keeping qualified employees requires a large cash outlay, especially when qualified individuals are scarce. Computer security will depend partly on how well those employees are supervised and motivated. One theory is that employees who know that their company values its security, reviews its practices, alters faulty programs, and punishes wayward employees as well as outsiders will be less likely to commit fraud and more likely to report it.

Security for system components should be commensurate with their value to the business. Total security is not possible; even attempting it would be prohibitively costly, as well as overly burdensome to users. Therefore, top management should be aware of the varying risks of computer information loss or modification. They should be part of the design and implementation of the security policy, with the security administrator reporting directly to senior management.

Chapter 2
Physical Security and
Data Preservation

The first line of defense for a computer system is to protect it physically: the plant, the equipment, and the personnel. Physical security protects the data, its integrity, accuracy, and privacy. An effective physical security system will prevent a security failure. However, should a system be successfully attacked, it should create an audit trail for investigators.

Computer equipment is at higher risk if it is easily accessible by the public or in a high crime area. And, of course, sometimes people authorized to be on your premises steal. The cost of theft can be very significant, far higher than the replacement price of the stolen equipment, because the company may also lose valuable data, especially if your work has not been properly backed up.

Computer Facilities

In the past, when computing tended to be centralized, it was easier to label a structure as the "computer center." With distributed computing, that is no longer possible. All areas where computing is done and from where an attack may be launched are vulnerable. Unauthorized access to computer facilities should be restricted through the use of surveillance equipment.

Facilities should be designed to protect computers, taking into account environmental factors like heating, cooling, dehumidifying, ventilating, lighting, and power systems. For example, the ducts of air conditioning units should be secured against access with heavy-gauge screens.

The following safeguards help protect computer facilities from both accidents and disasters like fire and floods:

- Adequate emergency lighting for safe evacuation in case of fire or other disaster.
- Fireproof containers to protect media (disks, tapes, or other output).
- User manuals for equipment and software to maintain continuity of proper operations.
- Surge protectors to protect the computer system against power line disturbances.

As computers become smaller, they can be housed in smaller areas and this changes the way facilities are designed. The layout of computer facilities is important in planning for computer security.

Central computer facilities should be housed near wire distribution centers but away from junctions of water or steam pipes. The room should be sealed tightly to minimize smoke or dust from outside.

Wire management is simple with multilevel computer racking furniture, which offers space flexibility and which is available from several suppliers:

- ACS Computer Network Racking Systems (*http://ourworld.compuserve.com/JLukach/*)
- Ergonomic Workstations Ltd. (*http://www.ergo-ws.com/*)
- Information Support Concepts (*http://www.iscdfw.com/*)
- LANSTAR (*http://lanstar.com/*)
- Page Concepts (*http://www.pagec.com/*)
- PC Innovations, Inc. (*http://www.pcinnov.com/*)
- Salix Group (*http://www.salixgroup.com/*)
- Stacking Systems, Inc. (*http://www.stackingsystems.com/*)
- Systems Manufacturing Corp. (*http://www.smcplus.com*)
- Workstation Environments (*http://www.workenv.com/*)

Roll-out shelves may be used for quick access to servers. Security cabinets should be used for controlled access to critical hardware and server systems.

If wiring is a concern, cables can generally be run along the walls. Racking shelves generally contain multistage openings for improved access to cables with a wide range of plugs and cable connectors.

Aluminum channels or I-beams can be used to raise components and cabinets if there is danger of flooding. Placing network equipment next to processing equipment can save cabling costs. Smaller components may be stacked vertically to conserve floor space and reduce cable costs. The Salix Group, for example, offers Spectro Data for networks; it is not limited by layout size and can be used for a high-capacity four-level configuration.

Multilevel units are cost-effective, and if they are ergonomically designed, productivity increases. The main work surface should provide vibration-free areas for screen, keyboard, and digitizing palette, with additional workspace for accessing other documents and equipment.

Americon (Stacking Systems, Inc.), for instance, offers server cabinetry for both active monitoring and closet environments. Its Network Solutions cabinetry may be used when floor space is at a premium. Its LAN Manager consoles allow for multiple stacking of servers, monitors, keyboards, and mice, along with desk surfaces and storage space. The LAN Commander cabinets contain these security features:

- Lock-in suspension glide shelving
- Seismic strapping for servers
- 180-degree rotating doors for access to both sides of the server
- Whisper-cool exhaust fans
- Heavy rated casters for moving from place to place
- Movement stabilization once the cabinet has been spotted
- Rear access through sliding doors

Optional accessories include:

- Remote access for consoles as far away as 250 feet
- Pullout server shelves
- EIA rack mounts for Ethernet equipment
- Induction fans for cooling when not on a raised floor

Workspace Resources (*http://www.workspace-resources.com*) provides design and marketing services for the office and contract furniture industry. It coordinates the needs of businesses with the capabilities of furniture manufacturers.

Environmental Considerations*

Computer facilities are susceptible to damage from a variety of environmental factors:

- *Heat* can cause electronic components to fail. Air conditioning is generally essential for reliable operation. Take simple precautions to ensure that air can circulate freely. Backup power should be available to air conditioning the computer system even if the primary power fails.

- *Water* is an obvious enemy of computer hardware. Floods, rain, sprinkler system activity, burst pipes, etc., can do significant damage. Check that water pipes are routed away from computer facilities. Instead of a traditional sprinkler system, consider using a less potentially harmful fire-extinguishing agent.

- *Humidity* at either extreme is harmful. High humidity can lead to condensation, which can corrode metal contacts or cause electrical shorts. Low humidity may permit the buildup of static electricity. The floors of computer facilities should either be bare or covered with anti-static carpeting. Monitor humidity continuously to keep it at acceptable levels.

- *Dust, dirt, and other foreign particles* can interfere with proper reading and writing on magnetic media, among other problems. Personnel should not be allowed to eat or drink around computers. The air should be filtered and the filters replaced regularly.

- *Power failure* can render all equipment useless. Brownouts and blackouts are the most visible sign of power failure. However, voltage spikes, which can cause serious damage, are much more common. Spikes like those produced by lightning may either damage equipment or randomly alter or destroy the data. A drop in line voltage can also lead to malfunction of computer equipment. Voltage regulators and line conditioners should be used if electricity fluctuates. Think about installing an uninterruptible power supply.

*Shim et.al., *Information Systems Management Handbook* (N.J.: Prentice-Hall, 1999).

Maintenance and Preventive Care

Regular maintenance can help prevent the unexpected downtime that can be caused by the weather and other environmental factors. Run diagnostic programs as part of regular maintenance and keep a maintenance log. You can quickly identify recurring problems by scanning the logs. At a minimum, log the following information:

- Type of equipment serviced
- Manufacturer and identification number of equipment serviced
- Date of service
- Services performed, including the results of diagnostic tests
- A note indicating whether the service was scheduled or not

Computer areas should be kept cleaned and dusted, with no eating, drinking, or smoking allowed. Set up programs to train your personnel in proper handling of computer equipment, peripherals, magnetic media, and CD-ROMs, reminding them of basic things like not putting magnetic media near telephones, radios, or other electric equipment, and writing labels before placing them on disks.

Set up a regular cleaning schedule for computers and peripheral equipment, and use cleaning products recommended by the manufacturer. Never spray electrical equipment directly with cleaning liquids. Clean keyboard surfaces with a damp cloth and vacuum with special computer vacuums.

Printers need to be cleaned to remove fibers, dust particles, and lint. Magnetic media devices, especially the read/write heads and transport rollers, can be cleaned with commercial products. Dust, smoke, fingerprints, and grease building up on recording surfaces can lead to crashes or permanent damage to the equipment and magnetic media.

Simple precautions, such as using static-resistant dust covers, can protect equipment, but never use them when the equipment is in use or it may overheat.

Water Alert Systems

Water alert systems should be installed wherever water might damage computer equipment, generally in the basement or in floors above the computer systems. Water sensing systems, which are especially useful in protecting electrical cables under the floor, should be installed within suspended ceilings and inside water-cooled computer cabinets and process cooling equipment. The water sensors should activate both an alarm and a drainage pump.

Static Electricity

Static electricity results from an excess or deficiency of electrons. An individual can easily become charged to several thousands of volts. While the current from electrostatic discharges is too low to harm humans, it can do a lot of damage to electronic equipment.

You can protect against electrostatic discharges by grounding, shielding, filtering, and limiting voltage. Vinyl flooring is generally better than carpeting to avoid static electricity buildup. Simple precautions can also minimize the dangers, such as:

- Using anti-static sprays
- Grounding computer equipment
- Using anti-static floor and table mats
- Maintaining a proper level of humidity

Humidity Control

Humidity should be tightly controlled. When air is too dry, static electricity is generated. When it is too high, above 80 percent, there may be problems with electric connections and a process similar to electroplating starts. Silver particles migrate from connectors onto copper circuits, thus destroying electrical efficiency. A similar process affects the gold particles used to bond chips to circuit boards. An optimal relative humidity level is 40 to 60 percent.

Wires and Cables

In distributed computing, it's essential to protect the wiring system. Generally there are two options for wires and cables, copper or optical fiber. While fiber optics offer significant performance and security advantages, they cost more to install. However, the cost disadvantage rapidly diminishes as the volume of data to be transferred increases.

Fiber optics work by sending light signals along very thin strands of glass or plastic fiber. The fiber's core is surrounded by cladding. The cladding causes the reflections, which guide the light through the fiber.

Two common types of fiber are multimode and singlemode. Multimode, which has a larger core, is used with LED sources for LANs.

Singlemode fiber, which has a smaller core, is used with laser sources. Plastic optical fiber has a much larger core; it uses visible light.

Cables and wires are fragile. A buffer coating protects the fiber from damage. Additional protection is provided by an outer covering, the jacket.

It is not possible to repair damaged wires; they must be replaced. In the process, the electrical properties of cables may be affected, in turn affecting the reliability of the data. Establish alternate paths for cables that are critical.

Fiber optics are more secure than copper. It is relatively easy for someone to tap copper lines if they can obtain access to them at any point. Such wiretaps are very difficult to detect. In contrast, it is much harder and more expensive to tap optical fibers. Moreover, normal operations are disturbed by a fiber optics tap, which can therefore be detected more easily. Yet even with fiber optics, a skilled person with proper equipment might tap the system undetected, so though fiber optics provides a deterrent to crime, they are not perfectly secure. Of course, the best way to protect sensitive data is to use encryption.

Fiber optics are not affected by electrical or magnetic interference. Copper wires have to be shielded with cabling and grounded metal conduits.

On the other hand, the ends of all fiber optic cables must be microscopically smooth. They have to be exactly aligned and positioned. This requires expensive special equipment and highly trained personnel.

An experienced person should certify any data wiring. The person should:

- Perform a visual inspection.
- Check that each cable is connected correctly.
- Check that there are no crossed pairs.
- Use a reflectometer to detect if there are any constrictions, bad terminations, or external interference.

Purchase orders for any wiring should specify:

- Who will certify the wiring.
- What equipment will be used to test the wiring.
- What standards will apply.

Protecting Information

The integrity, accuracy, and privacy of data are essential in any organization. Data lacks integrity if anything is:

- Missing
- Incomplete
- Inconsistent
- Poorly designed (in a database environment)

Data accuracy is not the same as data integrity. Data is accurate if

- It is reliable, and
- The data is what it purports to be.

Data privacy requires that only authorized individuals have access to data.

Destroying Data

Data that is no longer needed must be destroyed. Information on magnetic media is typically "destroyed" by overwriting on it. While this appears to destroy the information, there are many subtleties to consider. For example, if the new file is shorter than the old file, information may remain on magnetic media beyond the new file's end-of-file marker. Any information beyond that can be easily retrieved. Overwriting the entire medium is safer but time-consuming. Instead, use other methods, such as degaussing. Degaussers are essentially bulk erasure devices; when used within their specifications, they provide adequate protection.

Formatting a disk does not safely destroy all information. Magnetic media may retain a latent image of the preceding bit value after the writer insertion of a new bit value because it is not possible to completely saturate the magnetization. While normal read/write operations are not affected by this limitation, it does pose a security threat exploitable by anyone with sophisticated equipment.

Papers and other soft materials, such as microfiche and floppy disks, can be shredded. Some shredders cut in straight lines or strips; others cross-cut or produce particles. Some shredders disintegrate material by repeatedly cutting and passing it through a fine screen. Others may grind the material and make pulp out of it.

Burning is another way to destroy sensitive data. As with shredding, burning means that the storage medium can no longer be reused. Yet even with burning, you need to be careful. It's possible using special techniques, for example, to retrieve printed information from intact paper ashes, even though the information may no longer be visible to the human eye.

Controlling Access

Access controls guard against improper use of equipment, data files, and software. The oldest method of restricting physical access is with a lock. Locks are of two types, preset and programmable.

With *preset* locks, it's not possible to change the access requirements without physically modifying the locking mechanism. The combination on *programmable* locks, whether mechanical or electronic, can be more easily changed as security needs change, but their basic problem is that the entry codes are often easy for an observer to obtain. To overcome this problem, some electronic locks use a touch screen that randomly varies the digit locations for each user and restrict directional visibility to a perpendicular angle.

Make sure there's only one door for access into a secured access, and the entrance should not be directly from a public place. It should be self-closing and it shouldn't have a hold-open feature. A combination or programmable lock may be sufficient. Install an alarm system.

One development in access control combines security with asset management. For example, it's possible to link a laptop with a specific individual and detect when the asset is moved in, out, or within a facility.

Security guards and guard dogs can also be used to restrict access; their physical presence serves as a deterrent.

Pre-employment screening and bonding are essential when hiring security guards. Certain states, such as New York, have mandatory training requirements for guards.

The limitations of guards, however, are well-known. They can easily become bored with routine work and may not fulfill their duties as expected. It's easy for someone to forge identification to get past a guard. Through procedural error guards may also allow unauthorized individuals access to restricted areas.

Dogs have excellent hearing and a keen sense of smell. Guard dogs can be trained to "hold" intruders till security personnel arrive. On the other hand, security dogs mean you'll need additional liability insurance and training and maintaining dogs is expensive. Finally, they generally cannot differentiate between authorized and unauthorized visitors.

Still, security is enhanced if guards or dogs patrol the facilities often at random intervals. This psychological deterrence lets a potential intruder know that he might be caught. A determined attacker, of course, is unlikely to be bothered by psychological deterrents, so guards and dogs should always be backed up through other means.

Something as simple as lights can greatly enhance security. Lights make it easier for security personnel to carry out surveillance. Lights also make it harder for intruders to enter the facilities. Lights may be: left on all the time, put on timer or ambient control, activated by motion detectors, or manually operated.

To limit access a security system must be able to discriminate between authorized and unauthorized individuals. The three general discrimination methods are:

- *Identification*, comparing the physical characteristics of an individual with previously stored information. Access thus depends on who the person is. It may verify the individual's signature, personnel number, code, voice print, palm print, fingerprint, teeth print, or other personal trait. Secondary authentication, such as the user's place of birth, may be required for highly sensitive information.

- *User's name plus passwords* based on some combination of letters or numbers. There should be no logic to the password, so it cannot be easily guessed. Access depends on what the person knows. Passwords should be changed regularly; inactive passwords (e.g., more than four months old) should be deleted. When an employee leaves, block his password immediately. If a user changes a password, you'll need controls to prevent use of the old password. Passwords should not be shared. Access control software allows a minimum password time period in which a new password cannot be changed or a new password matching an old one will be rejected.

- *Cards/keys*. Access can depend on what a person possesses: Cards, keys, badges, etc. Improper access may be signalled by an alarm. Evaluate any unauthorized access pattern. You might want to look into smart cards, in which the user enters both an identification number and a randomly generated code that changes each time it's used or at stated times.

Computer and terminal access controls include:

- *Automatic shut-off:* The system signs off the user if the user fails to sign off after a transmission is completed.
- *Call-back:* A phone call is made to the terminal site to verify the user's identity before access is granted.
- *Time lock:* Access is denied to the system during specified hours, such as after normal business hours.

Within the plant, areas containing sensitive data should be accessible only to authorized personnel. These areas, including the computer rooms, should have only a single entry door that can be operated by an encoded magnetic ID card or by physical controls, such as a librarian keeping a log. A lockout should result from repeated errors.

Your logs should be automatic; they should list ID number, time of access, and function performed. Data dictionary software provides an automated log of access to software and file information. Use intrusion detection devices like cameras and motion detectors to monitor sensitive areas for the presence of unauthorized individuals.

Are your people diligently honoring the controls you're set up over processing, maintaining records, and file or software modification? Each individual function (e.g., accounts receivable, payroll) may require its own password so that users have access only to limited areas. The computer can keep an internal record of the date and time each file was last updated to compare against the log. The hours to access key files can be limited to prevent unauthorized access after normal working hours.

Files should be assigned different levels of confidentiality and security, such as Top Secret, Confidential, Internal Use Only, and Unrestricted. Confidential information should not be displayed on computer screens.

To control access to sensitive data, map access requirement to system components based on job function, with an appropriate segregation of duties. Temporary employees should be restricted to a specific project, activity, system, and time period. If you want to avoid possible data manipulation, don't give programmers free access to the computer area or the library. Keep those important disks locked up.

Hardware Security

While computer hardware has improved tremendously in reliability and speed, these technological advances have not always been good for computer security and data integrity.

Parity checks and data redundancies are critical for error-free data processing. Extra bits included at predetermined locations help catch certain types of errors when data is moved back and forth between different devices or from storage to registers.

- *Vertical redundancy checks (VRC)*, though common, have some problems. VRC are simple and inexpensive to implement. First, you determine whether there should be an odd or an even number of "1" bits in each character's binary code. An error is detected if the correct number is not transmitted. The basic flaw with the approach is that two errors may offset each other, allowing the error to go unnoticed. Furthermore, there is no standardization on the use of odd or even parity.

- *Longitudinal redundancy checks (LRC)* provide an additional safeguard since VRC may not detect all the errors. This technique involves the use of an extra character generated after some predetermined number of data characters. The bits in the extra character provide parity for its row. LRD has its limitations. It cannot correct multiple errors or errors in ambiguous position (ambiguous bit is correct for VRC but incorrect for LRD), or errors that do not result in both a VRC and LRC indication.

- *Cyclical redundancy checks (CRC)* are typically used when extra assurance of the accuracy of data is needed. A large number of redundant data bits is used, which requires longer transmission times and extra space in memory. The primary advantage of this technique is that any single error, whether in data bit or parity bit, would be detected.

Hardware typically has several features to protect the data during input, output, and processing.

- *Dual-Read* reads the same data twice and compares the two results. Any discrepancy indicates an error.
- *Read-After-Write* reads the data immediately after it's recorded to verify after it is recorded to verify the accuracy of the write function.

- *Echo Check* is used to verify the reception of a signal when data is transmitted to another computer or to peripheral devices such as printers.

- *Replication* is an important feature for critical applications. A backup computer/site is used in case of failure of the primary computer. Fault-tolerant or fail-safe computers contain at least two processors that operate simultaneously; if one fails, the other processors pick up the load. When a critical application requires extensive communication facilities, the backup equipment should contain both communication equipment and a processor. Repairs or replacement of malfunctioning equipment should be immediate.

- *Overflow* may result when an arithmetic operation, such as dividing by zero, results in values beyond a computer's allowable range. This function is typically built into the computer hardware.

- *Interrupts* are generated when the hardware detects deviations in order to maintain the integrity of the data processing system. For example, input/output (I/O) interrupts result when a previously busy device becomes available. The equipment then checks after each I/O interrupt to determine if the data has been written or read without error. I/O interrupts are generated when the Escape or Enter key is pressed. From a security perspective, interrupts can affect logs or cause the execution of unauthorized programs. Other types of interrupts include program check, machine check, and external. *Program check* interrupts terminate the program as a result of improper instructions or data. *Machine check* interrupts are generated by defective circuit modules, open drive doors, and parity errors. *External* interrrupts result from pressing an Interrupt key, from signal from another computer, or from timer action. From a security perspective, for example, the built-in electronic clock in the processor can be used to generate an interrupt at a specified interval to ensure that sensitive jobs do not remain on the computer long enough to be manipulated. Plan for the possibility of loss of data does not result because of interrupts.

Most integrated circuit chips on hardware equipment are inscrutable to a lay person. There are hundreds of thousands of transistors on a small semiconductor. Still, it's possible for a bug to be planted into electronic equipment, and it may be very difficult to detect. Several techniques may be used to seal hardware against such tampering.

Keep records of hardware failure and computer down times. Schedule regular maintenance, and record the results. If computer equipment needs frequent servicing, personnel might be tempted to bypass controls and take shortcuts, raising the possibility of human errors considerably. Analyze your records for unfavorable trends in downtime or frequently unscheduled service calls.

The hardware inventory logs for all computer equipment and peripherals should contain at least the following information:

- Description of the hardware
- Manufacturer's name
- Model number
- Serial number
- Company identification number
- Date of purchase
- Name, address, and phone number for the source of the item, whether store or manufacturer
- Date warranty expires
- Department or location where the hardware equipment will be used
- Name and title of individual responsible for the equipment
- Signature of the responsible individual or department head
- If the equipment is taken off premises, the date and time the equipment is checked out, and the date and time it's returned, along with the signature of the authorized individual

Hardware inventory logs should be stored in a secure location with a copy stored off-site. All hardware should be etched or engraved with the company name, address, telephone number, manufacturer's serial number, and company's identification number. To prevent theft, locking devices should secure computer equipment and peripherals to desktops, etc.

Software and Devices for Physical Security

A wide variety of software and devices is available to prevent computer theft. Computer Security Products, Inc. (*http://www.computersecurity. com*) provides an excellent assortment.

CompuTrace Theft Recovery Software

CompuTrace Theft Recovery Software is primarily for laptop computers, but it may be used with desktops. Once the software is installed, it works silently and transparently. Regularly and often, it uses the computer's modem to place a toll-free call to a monitoring center after checking to see if the modem is attached and in use. It turns off the modem speaker when making its scheduled call. The computer's serial number and the origination telephone number are recorded with each call.

If the computer is stolen, you call CompuTrace's theft hot line to acti-vate the Theft Recovery Assistance Procedure. The next time the stolen computer's modem dials in to the monitoring center, CompuTrace acquires the origination telephone number and determines its location. Local law enforcement authorities are then notified.

CompuTrace is available for DOS and Windows-based systems. It cannot be deleted; it even survives a hard-drive format. The only way to delete it is to use a registered copy of the uninstall disk.

CompuTrace, which uses less than 7K of memory is not detectable by antivirus software and does not appear in any directory. It's fully auto-mated and does not interfere with other applications.

It works from any phone line in North America. It works even if the phone number is unlisted. It doesn't rely on Caller-ID technology. It even works from hotel and office phones that require you to dial a prefix to reach an outside line. If CompuTrace doesn't detect a dial tone when it first calls out, it will try again with various prefix combinations.

Though CompuTrace's default calling schedule is usually 5 to 7 days, you may change it. It's also possible to program the computer to call in with greater frequency once it has been reported stolen. If the modem is not connected or is in use at the scheduled call time, CompuTrace keeps on trying periodically till the modem is available.

As an added benefit, CompuTrace may be used to manage computer assets in large organizations. The CompuTrace Monitoring Center pro-vides up-to-the-minute listings of all computers and their locations. It's easy to determine whether the computer is in a regional office, at an employee's home, or on the road. Monitoring reports can be downloaded from a private Internet web site. Reports can be distributed via email or fax.

CompuTrace is available from Computer Security Products, Inc. (800.466.7636). At the time of this writing, CompuTrace was available with:

- 1-year Monitoring Service for $89.95
- 2-year Monitoring Service for $149.95
- 3-year Monitoring Service for $199.95

Quantity discounts are available:

- 26—100 units   15%
- 101—250 units   20%
- 251—500 units   25%
- 501—1,000 units   28%
- over 1,000 units   30%

PC and Peripheral Security

Most computer equipment and peripherals can be quickly secured with steel cables, an easy and inexpensive theft deterrent. Special fasteners protect RAM chips and internal components. Cover locks can be used to:

- Lock the computer case
- Block access to disk drive slots
- Block access to the CD-ROM
- Block access to the on/off switch

The base of the cover lock can be attached to most flat surfaces. The locks may be keyed alike or differently. Master keying is also possible.

Lock-down plates provide additional security. The Cavalier Security System, for example, consists of two steel plates. The base plate contains the lock and is secured to a table. The insert or top plate is attached to the equipment to be protected. The plates come in various sizes depending on the width and length of the equipment to be secured. By selecting a size slightly smaller than the equipment's footprint, the lock-down plates appear less obtrusive.

Network Alarm

EtherLock Alarm System (*www.computersecurity.com*), which plugs into the hub, allows you to use your network as an alarm system. It interfaces with your existing alarm system and uses the network's wiring to secure computers; an alarm is triggered if a network wire is unplugged. It does not affect system performance or network throughput.

LockSoft Remote Management Software for EtherLock systems (*www.computersecurity.com/etherlock/locksoft.htm*) allows for control of the EtherLock system from any computer on the network. A central monitoring site can be notified of the attempted theft. Running LockSoft software with EtherLock lets you perform the following tasks from the central console:

- Receive network-based alarm reports when computers are disconnected.

- View the connection status of all protected devices.

- Remove individual devices from the protection loop for maintenance or relocation.

- Arm, disarm, and test all EtherLock systems connected to the network.

- Allow password-protected access to secure individual computers. This feature lets administrators give notebook users the flexibility to disconnect their machines.

At the time of this writing the cost of EtherLock 10T Base Unit was $1,948. The base unit can hold up to 16 Protection Modules, each costing $799 and supporting up to 12 devices. Therefore, the full system can protect up to 192 computers and peripherals on a single hub. Its modular design allows for expansion as the LAN grows. The minimum configuration requires one protection module.

The LockSoft software that comes with EtherLock computer security systems is available for Windows and DOS-based systems. Administrator software is included; it collects data on the EtherLock system and the devices being protected.

To protect laptop computers, the NoteLock security bracket ($19.95) may be used in conjunction with the EtherLock security system. You can connect to or disconnect from the network using the Ethernet cable. The LockSoft program simply asks you to enter a personal password. Personnel can be alerted if an attempt is made to remove a secured laptop computer from the network. Logging off from the network or powering down the computer does not affect the security features; only the appropriate password can be used to disconnect from the network.

The SimmLock security bracket ($19.95) is designed to protect memory chips (SIMMs), microprocessors, hard drives, and other internal components. Security personnel are alerted if any attempt is made to remove the computer case or access its internal components. SimmLock brackets can be affixed to monitors, external hard drives, and other peripheral equipment not directly connected to the network.

Asset Tracking

Tamper-proof asset-tracking security tags should be affixed on computers and peripherals. STOP (Security Tracking of Office Products) asset tags are available from Computer Security Products, Inc. (*http://www.computersecurity.com/stop/index.html*). Security plates or tags help in three ways: (1) they deter theft—a thief is less likely to steal tagged equipment; (2) they help in recovering stolen equipment; and (3) you can use these tags for asset management.

STOP plates link equipment data to a worldwide tracking and retrieval service. If equipment is lost or stolen, law enforcement authorities can be notified to track it. The barcode on STOP tags can be used to track equipment day to day and can interface with the Microsoft Access database.

The STOP security plate, made of photo-anodized aluminum, is secured to equipment using cyanoacrylate adhesive. It takes about 800 pounds of pressure to remove the security plate. If the plate is removed, the equipment casing will be noticeably altered.

Behind each plate is an indelible tattoo, "Stolen Property," that is chemically etched into the equipment. If someone succeeds in removing the security plate using special tools, the indelible marking is exposed, as are the company identification number (optional) and a toll-free number for verification and anti-theft information. This tattoo cannot be removed without defacing the case. Defacing is recognized by police and equipment sellers as a sign that the property is stolen.

Each security plate bears a warning that the property is monitored and traceable. It also warns that a tattoo has been etched into the equipment. Each plate also has a barcode to track information and a toll-free telephone number to call in case lost or stolen equipment is found.

Once equipment is registered, the STOP retrieval service will oversee its return. In any case of theft, STOP will help register the loss with law enforcement agencies in the United States and abroad.

STOP's hand-held barcode scanner, along with its asset tracking software, helps you maintain the inventory of valuable equipment. Inventory records are updated simply by scanning tags. The software will report on missing or out-of-plate hardware. It can also report on mobile equipment by registering who borrowed the equipment and when it was due.

The software is network-ready and customizable. It's based on the Microsoft Access database, but the software includes a runtime module, so Microsoft Access is not required to use the software. Source code is available for you to customize it.

Each STOP security plate costs $25. Quantity discounts can significantly reduce the cost of each plate. For example, if 10 or more plates are purchased, the price drops to $15 each. If more than 500 plates are ordered, the security plates cost less than $9 each. The Tattoo Activating Gel costs $2.50 for up to 10 security plates. For customized plates, the minimum order is 200 units and requires a one-time setup charge of $250.

The price of the security plate includes unlimited use for three years of STOP's anti-theft and retrieval hotlines and its recovery service.

After the first three years, unlimited use of these services costs $1 per year per machine, or $4 lifetime per machine. For large sites, a $200 flat fee per year covers an unlimited number of machines.

The STOP asset tracking management software costs $200 but is provided free with an order for 500 or more security plates.

The Intermec hand-held barcode scanner package costs $2,500 and includes:

- Communications dock and cable
- Charger
- Light wand and cord
- Power supply
- Barcode creation software
- STOP Asset Tracking Software

The Xyloc System

Xyloc access cards may be used to secure desktop computers and laptops. The card automatically locks the computer and blanks the screen when the authorized user with the card leaves a pre-defined area. It also automatically unlocks the computer system when the authorized user returns with the card. The computer's session work is preserved when the computer is locked. Background tasks continue to run even when the system is locked.

The pre-defined area, the "active zone," can be set from one to 50 feet. It allows access by many users to a single computer. Communication between the access card and the lock is encrypted to prevent an attacker from grabbing the code to create a clone. The system can be programmed to deploy incrementally to individual PCs, to workgroups, or enterprise-wide.

The Xyloc system is suitable when you need high security and restricted access to the computer system and system files. The system works either alone using the access card or, for even greater security, in conjunction with a password. On a LAN, it's possible to remotely manage several Xyloc systems from a central facility. The software maintains the audit trail and logs events. This information may be used, for example, to determine if proper security procedures are being followed.

The Xyloc key contains a low-power radio transceiver with a unique user identification code. It's powered by a lithium battery that typically lasts six months to a year. A battery meter lets you know how much power remains. The Xyloc Card Key is compatible with other ID and security badges. There's an encrypted channel for all communications with the lock.

The lock is a small device containing a low-powered transceiver. The lock simply plugs into the keyboard, serial, or USB port; it's powered by the port and contains a built-in status light.

The Xyloc Access Card system ($189.95; see *http://www.seattle-comp-sec.com*) consists of two pieces of hardware and software for the access control card. Each package includes one card key, one lock, and software. Additional pieces are available separately.

Card Technology

Many manufacturers are combining multiple technologies, such as bar codes, magnetic strips, proximity, and smart cards, on a single card. Such a card may also serve as a photo ID, which in effect gives it an additional function. A universal reader device that can support multiple formats will be required.

Current access control technology typically works by keeping doors locked. It denies access to everyone except those who can show or do something to get through the door. Technology is now proceeding in a new direction. Doors are left open, closing only when an unauthorized person tries to enter. For example, users might carry cards with chips that would tell the door that the person is an authorized user and that it's okay to stay open. The approach of anyone not carrying the appropriate card would close the doors.

There are potential problems associated with this technology. For example, assume a group of four people approaches. Only three of the four are authorized. The system should be capable of stopping the group and letting only the authorized individuals through.

Software for access control systems can help in collecting and managing a wide variety of data, data that could help determine, for example, the total amount of time spent on site by each cardholder. Access control data may be used to determine which employees are still in the facility during an emergency. This may save lives by helping authorities determine who might be trapped inside.

Visual Surveillance

Video surveillance is becoming increasingly popular. Cameras are more affordable. Image quality has improved tremendously. The components are getting smaller and more reliable. Cameras are more functional and responsive. Features such as panning, tilting, and zooming are common.

Digital videos, digital transmission of data, and digital storage are likely to increase the use of surveillance equipment. Digital storage allows security personnel to retrieve specific scenes quickly. Image quality tends to be much better than ordinary videotape.

Digital technology makes it possible to record and view images at the same time. Improvements in transmission media may mean that cameras at remote sites will replace more security officers. Remote monitoring and recording is becoming more feasible because of price decreases in components, including chips and memory.

Biometric Devices

Biometrics for access control purposes is on the horizon. It hasn't gained widespread popularity primarily because of its cost and lack of accuracy. Both are likely to diminish with improvements in computer processing. A facial recognition system for door access will soon be widely available. Companies are working on integrating fingerprint sensor technology into keyboards in order to restrict access to a terminal or a network. Miniature cameras at computer workstations may control access through facial recognition technology.

Chapter 3
Hardware Security

Software security depends on hardware security. If the hardware can be stolen or surreptitiously replaced, secure software will not help. Before the invention of the personal computer, computer mainframes were so huge that they took up an entire room. To secure these machines, IT managers locked the rooms. Now small and portable laptop and palmtop computers are easily stolen.

Companies use computers for storing sensitive information, doing online transactions, and accessing private and public networks. IT managers looking to protect their investments must consider securing the perimeter and allowing only authorized users access to their computers.

Some hardware problems are common:

- Equipment and removable media can be stolen or substituted.
- Changing hardware setup parameters can circumvent security.
- Systems can be booted by unauthorized users or unauthorized software.
- Boot media can be rewritten by unauthorized software.
- Unauthorized software can be executed from removable media.

Some of the safeguards that can be taken are:

- Locking doors and security equipment
- Having lockable cases and keyboards and removable media drives
- Having a key or password-protected configuration and setup
- Requiring a password to boot
- Requiring a password to mount removable media

- Using read-only media
- Storing removable media in secured areas

Organizations that store and transmit sensitive and valuable information over both public and private networks should be concerned with information security (see Figure 3.1). For example, security breach can occur in hardware, software, network connections, or authentication procedures. Today, securing information is more difficult not only because PCs are portable but also because of cheap high-speed modems and the Internet. Attacks are becoming more sophisticated. Hackers have tools to automate attacks.

FIGURE 3.1: CSI/FBI 1998 Computer Crime and Security Survey

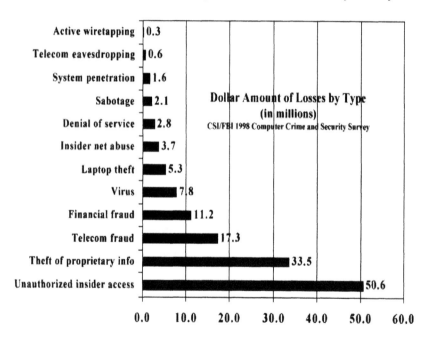

Source: Computer Security Institute

Security breaches cost companies millions of dollars not only in losses but also in increased staff hours, decreased productivity, loss of credibility in the marketplace, and legal liability. Of 520 companies surveyed in the 1998 Computer Security Institute/FBI Computer Crime and Security Survey, 64% reported a security breach. The total financial loss for that 64% was estimated at over $136 million. These figures are very conservative; they do not reflect corporations that did not realize they had a security breach or those that are reluctant to report one for fear of negative press.

Note particularly in Figure 3.1 that $50.6 million in financial losses were attributable to unauthorized insider access.

Physical Security

Physical security is almost everything that happens before a user (or an attacker) starts typing commands on the keyboard. Surprisingly, many organizations are not deeply concerned about physical security. It may be the form of security most likely to be forgotten because physical security threats, practices, and protections are different for practically every site (Garfinkel, 1996).

Yet, physical security is not that hard:

- Access should only be given to those who need specified data.
- Computer rooms should have bars on any windows or electronic detection devices as needed.
- Access to rooms containing computers should be restricted to specific personnel. These rooms can be controlled with locked doors, posted guards, and similar restraints.
- Protect computers with lockable equipment enclosures, lockable power switches, fasteners, and other securing devices.
- Make sure other electronic devices do no interfere with computers, and that the computers do not interfere with other electronic devices.
- Keep computers in a comfortable environment to prolong their life and ensure the safety of stored data.
- Shield computers from sudden surges or drops in electrical line voltage with surge protectors or uninterruptible power supplies.

Data Integrity

Data integrity is as important as the actual hardware. Data integrity refers to the validity of data. If integrity is compromised, there is no point in protecting your data. Data integrity can be compromised in a number of ways:

- Human errors when data is entered
- Errors occurring when data is transmitted between computers
- Software bugs or viruses
- Hardware malfunctions, such as disk crashes
- Natural disasters, such as fires and floods

To minimize threats to data integrity:

- Back up data regularly.
- Control access to data.
- Design user interfaces that prevent the input of invalid data.
- Use error detection and correction software when transmitting data.

Network Backup

In a world where intruders can come from both inside and outside, IT managers need a contingency plan to make sure that if an intruder sabotages an entire system, they can bring the data back. Backing up data to a network backup server is critical. Having a centralized backup location can save you time and money searching for backup tapes. Organizations that support heterogeneous clients also need this capability.

Retrospect Remote 3.0 from Dantz Development Corp. is a full-featured backup server. With the Remote Pack 1.0 client software running on a dedicated Macintosh, it can back up Windows as well as Macintosh clients, handling all backup, restore, duplication and backup server tasks, whether client sources are hard drives, external or removable media, or files in subdirectories (Windows) or folders (Mac).

Access Control System

Consider securing the perimeter of your building. By allowing only unauthorized users access to your facility, you greatly reduce the risk of someone stealing proprietary information.

RAND Corporation, a respected nonprofit policy research organization, controls physical security with staff access cards, alarms, surveillance cameras, and its own guard force. Surveillance cameras record all entrances to and exits from the building, including the entire parking lot. The guards screen, sign in, and escort visitors to their destinations and patrol both interior and perimeter of the facility. They investigate incidents and complaints and may escort staff to their cars. Only RAND staff members are allowed in the facility.

Memory Data Integrity Checking

Ensuring the integrity of data stored in memory is an easy way to make sure your data is secured before being saved to floppy disk or on the network. Consider buying computers that use data integrity checking to prevent later errors. Especially for computers with critical roles, such as servers, an error correction code (ECC) capable memory controller is a good idea.

The two primary methods to ensure the integrity of data stored in memory are parity and ECC. Parity is the most common: One bit is added to every 8 bits (1 byte) of data. The limitation is that the parity method can detect an error but cannot correct it. ECC is more comprehensive: It can correct as well as detect 1-bit errors, usually without the user even knowing that there has been an error. Kingston (*www.kingston.com*), an independent manufacturer, sells data integrity checking memory products for use in workstations, servers, desktops, portables, and printers.

Deploying a Security System

When planning a security system, form a strategy rather than randomly deploying gizmos. Three possible strategies are perimeter security, interior security, and physical protection of individual assets. While you want to keep intruders out, you also want to limit the amount of damage they can do once they are inside.

Perimeter Security

Perimeter security means preventing entry by criminals, who choose the easiest points, usually doors and windows. Windows can be protected with small, easily mounted devices that sound an alarm when the glass is broken.

Access control systems are complex, high-tech information networks but they are essential to office security. Authorization can take many forms, including entering a code into a keypad, sliding a card through a scanner, or pressing a button on a wireless remote control. ADT, an electronic security company, sells access control systems like a card reader (see Figure 3.2) to help companies track the comings and goings of their employees.

FIGURE 3.2: ADT Card Reader

Source: ADT

Interior Security

Interior security is as much about deterring intruders as about catching them. Motion detectors can be used to set off alarms. Surveillance cameras can detect theft when they are located so as to catch the intruder's eye. Deltavision (*www.deltavision.com*), a Canadian CCTV manufacturer, sells a wall or ceiling-mounted camera that interfaces with Deltavision recorders for 24-hour real-time surveillance (see Figure 3.3). If you're worried about espionage, you can buy cameras disguised as clocks, telephones, or even exit signs.

FIGURE 3.3: Deltavision designer mount camera

Source: Deltavision

Physical Protection of Individual Assets

Many computing devices are small enough to be put in a briefcase and carried away. Cable kits can be an inexpensive solution to this problem. Some hardware devices can be connected to computers and set to trigger an alarm. Software can be installed in a laptop to let police track down stolen laptops.

Integrated Firewall Appliances

For IT managers looking for strong security without any impact on network performance, Cisco Systems, Inc. (*www.cisco.com*), the worldwide leader in networking for the Internet, provides the PIX Firewall Series. Unlike typical CPU-intensive proxy servers that perform extensive processing on each data packet, a PIX Firewall uses a non-UNIX, secure, embedded system. Its performance of up to 256,00 simultaneous connections, over 6,500 connections per second, and nearly 170 megabits per second (Mbps) throughput is dramatically greater than that delivered by other appliance-like firewalls or those based on general-purpose operating systems.

The PIX series is based on the adaptive security algorithm (ASA), which effectively protects access to the internal host network by comparing inbound and outbound packets to entries in a table. Access is permitted only if passage can be validated. Cut-through proxy, which enhances authentication, challenges a user initially at the application later, but once the user is authenticated and policy is checked, the PIX Firewall shifts session flow to a lower layer for dramatically faster performance. PIX

Firewalls allow you to accommodate thousands of users without affecting performance.

Total VPN Solution

In the software security chapter, it will be shown that companies rely on virtual private networks (VPN) to allow telecommuters, customers, suppliers, and branch offices access their internal information. Unfortunately, VPN security software requires extensive encrypting, with decrypting at the server end, which means that users experience performance degradation. As your organization grows and more people use VPN, performance of the host computer will be further impeded.

Chrysalis-ITS, Inc. (*www.chrysalis.com*), the provider of high-performance network security solutions, now offers a hardware solution, Luna VPN. Luna VPN extends security network connections across Intranet, Extranet, and Internet by combining security software and hardware acceleration into one package. With Luna VPN hardware, the encryption and decryption processing is offloaded from the host computer to increase network throughput and remove bottlenecks. The Luna VPN combination increases performance by up to 11 times for DES operations, and up to 19 times for Triple-DES operations (Figure 3.4).

FIGURE 3.4: Luna VPN Network Throughput Performance

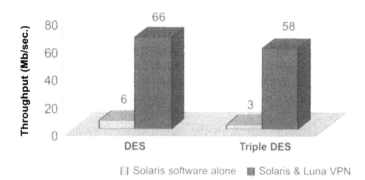

Source: Security Assurance White Paper from Chrysalis-ITS, 1999

Processor overhead can also be decreased when Luna VPN is added, because it can significantly offload the host CPU. Adding a second processor to either Solaris or Windows NT systems does not offload processing from the host processor as effectively.

Notebook Security

As computer theft and network break-ins become a growing concern for notebook users and their companies, major computer vendors are offering products to safeguard their machines:

- *IBM* offers a Smart Card Security Kit on its notebooks' hard drives.
- *HP* offers smart cards on its OmniBook notebooks, Vectra desktop PCs, and Kayak workstations.
- *Dell* offers a hard-drive password feature on Latitude notebooks, OptiPlex desktops, and Precision workstations.
- *Compaq* uses Fingerprint Identification Technology (biometrics instead of passwords) to log on to a network on its Deskpro, Armada, and Professional Workstation systems.

Smart-card technology offers numerous security advantages:

- Users can log in from any PC on the network, enabling "roaming" between PCs and easy import of temporary or flex-time personnel.
- A digital signature on the card provides instant proof of sender identity and message authentication.
- Permanent encryption keys ensure that stored information is transmitted easily without compromising confidentiality.
- Chip circuitry for smart cards is tamper-proof, becoming void upon exposure to light.
- Sensitive information is stored on the card itself, unlike biometrics user-authentication systems, which store data within a system database, where it might be accessed illegally.
- Smart cards can display an employee's identification photograph and double as a swipe card for entry to company facilities.

Tokens: Dual-Factor Security

It's not hard for a sophisticated hacker or a determined insider to gain access to a supposedly secure system if your confidential resources are protected only with a single factor, a user password. Security Dynamics Technologies, Inc. (*www.securitydynamics.com*), has developed a SecurID token for a two-factor identification. Factor one is something secret that only the user knows, such as a PIN or a password. The second factor is something the user possesses, the SecurID token, a small device the size of a credit card that displays a constantly changing ID code (Figure 3.5).

FIGURE 3.5: SecurID Token

Source: Security Dynamics

The SecurID is a microprocessor-based handheld device that generates unique, one-time, unpredictable access codes every 60 seconds. To gain access, a user must enter a name, a personal identification number, and the code currently displayed on the SecurID token. The security server compares the code with the proper password for that time period. The tokens require no card readers or time-consuming challenge/response procedures.

The tamperproof SecurID token can:

- Prevent unauthorized access to information resources
- Authenticate users at network, system, application, or transaction level

- Be used from any PC, laptop, or workstation—ideal for remote access and VPNs
- Work seamlessly with WebID for secure Web access
- Work across access control modules (ACMs) for multiple platform enterprise security

Securing sensitive data is especially important when it involves access to clinical data. Beth Israel Deaconess Medical Center in Boston uses the SecurID token to authenticate access to its medical databases. When Beth Israel Hospital and Deaconess Medical Center merged in October 1996, the SecurID token gave them a single way with an identical look and feel to get on both systems: Beth Israel stores its patient records in a custom-built Mumps-based system, while Deaconess uses a Sybase repository (Harrison, 1999).

The hospitals looked at other security tools like biometrics but the hardware would have had to be deployed on every PC. They were concerned with error rates caused by a greasy fingertip, which could lock a medical worker out of access to urgently needed medical data. The hospitals are now looking at smart cards to consolidate applications that currently include swipe cards, digital certifications, VPN, and tokens.

The SecurID token is interoperable with Cisco and Intel routing products and compatible with VPNs. Some users may send authentication passwords remotely over public networks.

The Smart Card

A smart card is a credit-card-sized device that has an embedded microprocessor, a small amount of memory, and an interface that allows it to communicate with a workstation or network. According to the Smart Card Industry Association, some 1.6 billion smart cards were issued in 1998. In 2000, that number is expected to be 2.8 billion. The most common application is the phone card, which stores a set value for use in public pay phones (see Table 3.1).

With smart cards, passwords and Ids are securely encrypted on the card; when combined with biometrics finger-scanning technologies, users can even skip the PIN code.

Table 3.1: Smart Card Applications and Projected Growth Rates
by Units Deployed

Application Cards Issued Smart Card Applications	In Cards Issued 1996 (millions)	In Cards Issued 2000 (millions)	In Annual Average Growth Rate (%)
Pay phone	605	1,500	29
GSM	20	45	25
Health care	70	120	14
Banking	40	250	105
Identity/access	20	300	280
Transportation	15	200	247
Pay TV	15	75	80
Gaming	5	200	780
Metering/vending	10	80	140
Retail/loyalty	5	75	280

Source: Smart Card Industry Association

A smart card can be personalized to the user. For example, a company using smart cards to provide access to network services would store network privileges and preferred system settings on each employee's card, which could then be used from any terminal with a card reader, customizing the desktop to the employee's preference.

Two characteristics make smart cards especially well-suited for security-sensitive or personal data applications:

1. The onboard processor can service requests from the network and return the results without divulging the sensitive data. For example, a smart card could digitally sign data without divulging the user's private key.

2. The user can carry data on the smart card rather than entrusting it to network storage. For example, a smart card could be used to carry personal information about the user, such as medical records or digital certificates.

Microsoft Windows NT4.0, Windows 95, and Windows 98 all support smart cards and smart card readers based on specifications established by the Personal Computer Smart Card (PC/SC) Workgroup of leading companies. Windows-compatible smart card solutions can be used with Internet Explorer to authenticate a secure connection and with Outlook Express or Outlook 98 for sending and receiving secure e-mail.

Through the use of public key cryptography and X.509 certificates, smart cards securely store private as well as public key certificates. Embedded private key is the digital certification representation of a user's identify. Smart card allows you to digitally sign and encrypt messages, provides access to protected Intranet sites, and can enable a single network sign-on (Backman, 1999).

Two-Factor Authentication

Security Dynamics Technologies, Inc. offers two-factor authentication technology in a smart card version for use on corporate Intranets. As with the SecurID token, its design incorporates a PIN number and a unique password. The smart card version, the SecurID 100, however, will generate the unique password automatically and transmit it to the server without any user involvement. The same card could be used to gain access to the facilities or store value for use in company cafeteria and vending machines.

With the SecurID 1100 smart card, you can customize features to provide building access by incorporating magnetic stripes or holograms. The card can be combined with corporate employee badge systems and other security applications. Other applications can be integrated with the smart card to customize it to your own environment.

Smart Cards in Banks

Guarding the privacy of bank customers requires the strongest possible security. One company that believes smart cards can provide a high level of protection is the Union Bank of Switzerland (UBS), among the largest banks in the world. As of March 1999, UBS had deployed 12, 500 smart cards among its employees and was adding about 1,000 per month. Employees use the smart cards to gain access to the company network and files. Eventually UBS plans to deploy smart cards to all 35,000 of its Swiss employees.

Because the UBS network is decentralized, it did not fit well with server-based authentication solutions. Smart cards, however, allow for authentication and a single sign-on (SSO). Schumann Security Software, Inc. (*www.shumannsoftware.com*), offers the Secure Single Sign-On (SAM/SSSO) to deliver strong authentication and confidential data transfer. Unlike other systems, SAM/SSSO does not require a central authentication server. It uses DES encryption and RSA-based public key infrastructure (PKI). The General Security Service (GSS) API (*www.gssc.net*) provides the common interface between the smart card and secured applications. Where strong authentication has not been added to an application, the smart card also supports conventional log-in via a script engine that automatically logs on with a user ID and password stored in the smart card.

The basic components of SAM/SSSO are a smart card and a smart card reader. User log-ins and passwords are stored on a tamper-proof smart card and are accessible only with a single sign-on PIN for off-site as well as on-site security. With SAM/SSSO hours of wasted productivity spent in changing or losing passwords can be avoided.

UBS's smart card single sign-on process starts when the user enters smart card, ID, and password into the reader (Figure 3.6). The user clicks on the desired application, triggering the scripting engine to launch the application script, which may be on the workstation or the network server. The script delivers the ID and password from the smart card to the application log-on screen.

FIGURE 3.6: UBS's Smart Card Single Sign-On

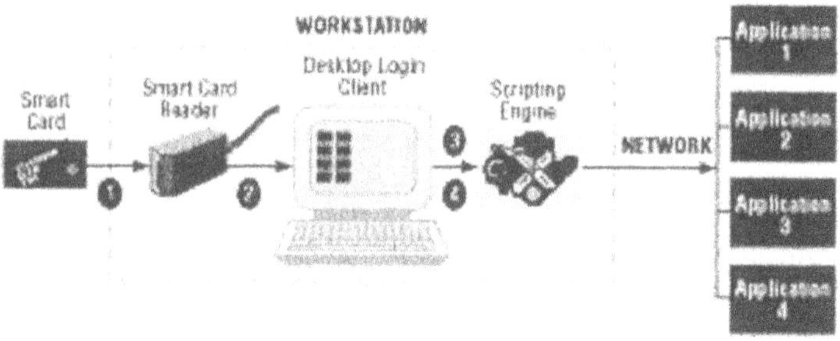

Source: Information Security Magazine, 1999

Smart Card Vulnerabilities

While the flexibility of smart cards gives them many uses for businesses—access control, e-commerce, authentication, privacy protection—it can also be susceptible to attacks. Think about the following vulnerabilities of smart cards:

- Attacks by the cardholder
  - Against the terminal
  - Against the data owner
  - Against the issuer
  - Against the software manufacturer
- Attacks by the terminal owner against the issuer
- Attacks by the issuer against the cardholder
- Attacks by the manufacturer against the data owner

IT managers can prevent these attacks if they use both a smart card and a portable smart card reader from one vendor. Cylink Corporation, (*www.cylink.com*), an ISO 9001-certified provider of encryption-based network security solutions to Fortune 500 companies, provides an advanced public key smart card, the PrivateCard, and a smart card reader, PrivateSafe. Using them in combination, you can be assured that sensitive private information never leaves the card.

The PrivateCard Smart Card is an isolated tamper-proof smart card with an onboard microprocessor and control program. The user's digital signature public and private key pair is produced on the card and never leaves it. Since all sensitive private key cryptographic functions are performed securely on the smart card chip, it protects the private key from attacks and prevents exposure to a potentially hostile external environment. PrivateCard can be integrated with other security products.

PrivateCard has the following features:

- *RSA key generation* supports up to 1,024-bit RSA functions.

- *Random number generation* is preformed inside the smart card chip itself.

- *RSA private key functions* such as decrypt and digital signatures are all performed on-chip.

- *Multiple keys and data objects* may be stored on the card.

- Authorized users can perform *access control and PIN management* securely.

- *Passwords* can be changed after a specified period.

- *Multiple-level file system* allows information to be secured by directory.

The PrivateSafe Smart Card Reader connects between the keyboard and the PC (see Figure 3.7); no additional hardware or external power supply is needed. Bypassing keyboard input, PrivateSafe isolates the user's private information on the smart card so that it never reaches the PC. It generates the public key pairs right on the PrivateCard so that the user's private key is never exposed to the PC.

FIGURE 3.7: PrivateSafe Smart Card Reader

Source: Cylink Corporation

Tokens

A token is a small device no bigger than a credit card that displays a constantly changing ID code. Once the user enters a password, the card displays an ID that can be used to log into a network. As an alternative to entering an ID code from a token or deploying a smart card reader, Aladdin Knowledge Systems (*www.aks.com*), an information security company, has developed eToken (see Figure 3.8), a car-key-sized token that plugs into a computer's Universal Serial Bus (USB) port (a standard feature on virtually all PCs and laptops manufactured since 1997). USB provides true "plug and play" for up to 127 peripherals.

FIGURE 3.8: Aladdin's eToken

Source: Aladdin Knowledge Systems

Flexible enough to hold information without an expensive reader, eToken contains its own processor chip to encrypt information; store private keys, passwords, digital certificates, and digital cash; and provide two-factor authentication for secure access to VPNs, remote access servers, subscription-based Web content, and back office applications.

Aladdin's eToken technology opens and guards doors in e-commerce, e-banking, VPNs, Extranets, and WANs. It can protect sensitive data and resources with file encryption and access control, and it can sign or encrypt electronic messages so that they cannot be forged, changed, or intercepted.

eToken has the following features:

- *Easy to use:* No additional hardware or software is needed. You just insert eToken into the USB port on a desktop, laptop, monitor, or keyboard and type in a password.

- *Cost-effective:* The cost is between $20 and $50 per token, depending on the size of the setup.

- *Compact and convenient:* Only the size of a car key, eToken is portable.

- *Highly secure:* Credentials are stored in a tamper-proof container, providing a higher degree of security than software-only solutions.

- *Versatile:* eToken can contain a large number of private keys for different applications.

Biometrics

Biometrics identifies people based on unique physical characteristics or behavioral traits using body features such as fingerprints, eyes, or faces, and ways of doing things, such as speaking or writing signatures. The catalyst for biometrics is the growing realization that passwords can get lost, misplaced, forgotten, or written on notes and stuck on computer monitors for anyone to use. Valuable corporate data is often compromised as a result.

Biometric technology has not yet gained wide acceptance. Of the $100 billion spent on private security, Mentis Corp., a market research firm in Durham, NC, says, the biometric market totaled only $100 million in 1999. Mentis predicts, however, that the market will grow from 27% to 35% through 2000 as pattern-recognition software improves, computers become better able to handle biometric applications, and prices fall.

The term "biometrics product" has multiple definitions:

- A component that captures a human characteristic
- Associated hardware
- Application software
- Image-matching software
- A stand-alone product
- A complete solution
- A platform or environment that supports biometric authentication

This technology is still expensive without being as effective as other security products. Moreover, people see having their eyeballs scanned as an invasion of privacy. They fear a Big Brother-like agency keeping tabs on fingerprints and voiceprints. Once they understand how limited the data needed is, they are likely to become more comfortable with the technology.

Some of the commercially available biometric identification methods are (see Table 3.2):

- *Voiceprint:* Sound waves generated by an individual speaking a given word or password are compared to stored patterns.
- *Fingerprints:* Ridges on fingers are converted to a digital template that can be compared with database records.

- *Palm prints:* The ridges of the palm are measured for comparison with a database.

- *Hand geometry:* Measures the size and shape of the hand.

- *Hand veins:* The vein pattern on the back of the hand is scanned, creating a digital template that can be matched against stored patterns.

- *Handwriting acoustic emissions:* Analyzes sounds generated when a person signs his or her name.

- *Iris map:* A video image of the colored portion of the eye is mapped by computer, creating a digital code based on the individual pattern of the iris.

- *Facial thermographs:* Use an infrared camera to capture heat emission patterns; there is a unique signature when heat passes through facial tissue.

- *Facial identification:* Converts a video image of the face to a digital template to be compared with a recorded image.

TABLE 3.2: Common biometric techniques and how they rate

	User Criteria		System Criteria	
	Intrusiveness	**Effort**	**Accuracy**	**Cost**
Dynamic signature verification	Excellent	Fair	Fair	Excellent
Face geometry	Good	Good	Fair	Good
Finger scan	Fair	Good	Good	Good
Hand geometry	Fair	Good	Fair	Fair
Passive iris scan	Poor	Excellent	Excellent	Poor
Retina scan	Poor	Poor	Very good	Fair
Voice print	Very good	Poor	Fair	Very good

Source: International Biometric Group, New York

Generally, biometric authentication is a two-phase process. The first is scanning personal characteristics of users, such as fingerprints irises, faces, signatures, or voiceprints, into the computer. Key features are then converted to unique templates, which are stored in the computer as encrypted numerical data. In the second phase, the user presents that personal characteristic and the computer compares it with the template in the database. But in the real world, matches will rarely be perfect due to extraneous factors and background interference.

Voiceprint

With VoiceGuardian from Keyware Technologies (*www.biometrics.org*), provider of Layered Biometric Verification solutions, the enrollment process consists of repeating a pass phrase three times. An example would be "My voice is my password." The voiceprint may be stored on the security server, smart card, or local PC. The second stage of verification is accomplished by speaking the pass phrase one time; the live voice sample is then evaluated against the stored voiceprint. If the voiceprint is accepted, the user can access the secure resources.

Authentication is performed through analysis by a verification engine of an individual's speech patterns at the phoneme level, looking for the points of inflection and articulation that form a unique voice pattern. Although users do not consider voiceprint as intrusive, its accuracy currently is only fair.

Fingerprint

Your fingerprints have unique characteristics such a whorls, arches, loops, ridge endings, and ridge bifurcations. Verification systems capture the flat image of a finger and perform one-to-one verification. Compaq Computer Corp. (*www.compaq.com*) uses Fingerprint Identification Technology to simplify the log-in process (see Figure 3.9). Compaq claims that up to 50 percent of calls to corporate help desks are related to forgotten or expiring passwords. Furthermore, passwords can be duplicated, forged, or stolen. Compaq's Fingerprint Identification Technology makes two connections to your PC, one between the keyboard and the PC and the other to the parallel port. It uses software algorithm technologies to convert the image into a unique map of minutiae points.

Minutiae points are unique data points that describe the fingerprint. The encrypted map, rather than the actual fingerprint, is stored within the network (see Figure 3.10). Since you cannot recreate the fingerprint from the data, your fingerprint image is never stored anywhere on the network.

FIGURE 3.9: Compaq Fingerprint Identification Technology

Source: Compaq Computer Corporation

FIGURE 3.10: Minutiae Points

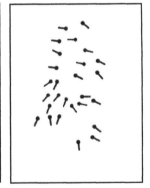

| **Finger Image** | **Finger Image & Minutiae** | **Minutiae** |

Source: Compaq Computer Corporation

An authorized user only has to register those unique minutiae points once to the server to set up a digital record. To get logged on to the network, the user only has to place the registered finger on the reader attached to his or her PC. Fingerprint Identification Technology is compatible with both Windows 95 and Windows NT Workstation 4.0.

Since fingerprint authentications are unique, not easily copied, and relatively inexpensive, they are more likely to have widespread use than other biometric solutions. Fingerprints can be used in a wide range of applications, such as the Internet e-commerce, credit card, and ATM authentication. Once the cost of biometric systems comes down enough and standards mature, for many passwords may well become a thing of the past.

Iris Recognition

Your iris, the colored portion of your eye, is one of a kind. Even your own right and left iris patterns are completely different. Each iris contains more than 266 measurable discriminators (a fingerprint contains about 35) (see Figure 3.11). Moreover, the iris remains stable, protected, and virtually unchanged from 18 months of age until death.

FIGURE 3.11: Iris Identification

Source: Sensar Inc.

Although the biometric identifier such as an iris offers the convenience of not having to carry a photo ID and various cards, keys, and codes, some people worry that we are moving toward a world where the price of convenience is our personal privacy. The public considers iris scan technology as intrusive because the camera is taking a picture of one's eye.

The two types of iris recognition systems are *active* and *passive*. The active system must be manually focused and the user must be close to the camera. The price of the active iris scan system is several thousand dollars, including the camera and the software necessary to run the application on the PC.

The passive system is substantially easier to use: It incorporates a set of cameras to automatically locate the user's face and eye, removing the need to manually focus the camera. Passive iris scan is the most expensive biometric technology—it costs tens of thousands of dollars—because the technology, available only for a few years, has not yet been mass-produced.

The passive Sensar Iris Identification System (see Figure 3.12) uses three video cameras to get a high-quality image from as far away as three feet. It maps the iris and converts it into a digital bar code in less than two seconds. The system consists of two modules, the Identification Optical Platform and the Identification Process Platform, connected by a cable up to 10 feet long. Sensar claims that the matching probability of the Iris Identificaiton System is greater than that of DNA testing.

FIGURE 3.12: Iris Identification System

Source: Sensar Inc.

Bank United, the largest bank headquartered in Texas, is the first bank in the United States to introduce Iris Recognition ATMs. Thousands of consumers in Houston, Dallas, and Fort Worth can withdraw cash from their accounts at the ATM just by looking at it; the camera will instantly photograph the customer's iris. If the iris data matches the record stored at the time of enrollment, access will be granted. Positive identificaiton can be read through glasses, contact lenses, and most sunglasses. As more people rely on iris recognition and as the prices fall, we are likely to see more use of this technology.

Face Recognition

Your face is yours alone. Securing your computer network through face recognition makes it easy to unlock access to your company's applications and data. Miros Inc. in Wellesley, MA, (*www.miros.com*) provides TrueFace Network (see Figure 3.13), which incorporates neural network recognition technology with True-Face Isolator, the first automated neural network face location.

FIGURE 3.13: TrueFace Network

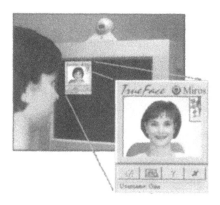

Source: Miros Inc.

Selecting a Biometric System

Many applications of biometrics are in use today. Before deciding on whether to use biometrics in your organization, review the following steps recommended by the Biometrics Consortium (*www.biometrics.org*):

- Identify the level of security in the current application, measuring five basic parameters.
  1. Total elapsed time taken for enrolling a person
  2. Total elapsed time taken by an individual to successfully use the application
  3. Percentage of false rejections
  4. Percentage of false acceptances

5. Uniformity of performance of the application across the population who will use the application

- What improvements are required in the future application for each of the five parameters? Define the target figures for the new application.

- Select a biometric and a manufacturer (lists of reputable manufacturers are available from the Biometrics Consortium).

- Perform a "black box" screening test run by your own employees or an independent consultant to see how well the biometric device performs against your defined parameters.

- Implement the biometric fully, with integration, implementation, planning, and testing.

Questions to be answered:

- Biometric type
  - How suitable is the biometric to the application?
  - Are there any persons or groups who cannot use the biometric?
- Biometric device
  - Is the price of the device likely to fit the proposed budget?
  - Is the size of the biometric device significant?
- Biometric manufacturer
  - What is the reliability, quality of service, and reputation of the manufacturer?
  - Who are the manufacturer's major clients?
- Fraud potential
  - Can the application be cheated if the criminal learns as much about the application as the manufacturer knows?
  - If the biometric is used for verification, can the token be forged easily?

Remote Access Security

Banks of modems have typically provided users remote access to corporate networks by dialing through the public switched telephone network. This is expensive in terms of equipment, support costs, and the cost of telecommunications service. With the Internet, companies can dramatically reduce their remote access costs by implementing VPN technology that fosters business-to-business integration.

Extending your network to the outside world raises the question of how to protect network security and data integrity. Contivity Extranet Switch 2500 from Bay Networks (*www.nortelnetworks.com*) provides secure Extranets for business partners and secure connectivity for remote users, yet with industrial-strength remote access for corporate travelers and trading partners. It also provides the functionality, performance, and security of a secured Extranet.

Contivity Extranet Switch 2500 has the following benefits:

- *Cost-effective:* You can leverage the cost by using the Internet as the network infrastructure to provide a secure Extranet at both the central site and the branch office.

- *Flexible and easy to use:* Designed as a "plug and play" device, it allows you to work with existing network infrastructure components such as routers, firewalls, and authentication servers.

- *High performance:* It's designed with all the hardware and software necessary to support VPN tunnels, encryption, compression, and filters for up to 400 simultaneous active users.

- *Flexible security:* The security architecture is integrated but ensures that only authorized users can access the network.

- *Standards-based technology:* It supports constantly changing VPN and Extranet technology standards.

- *High availability:* It allows up to 400 simultaneous users.

- *Flexible management:* It's fully configurable from any browser using HyperText Markup Language (HTML) and Java configuration and monitoring.

- *Broad client support:* It supports industry-standard PPTP clients from third parties.

Contivity Extranet Switch 2500 supports leading certificate authorities such as Entrust; radius providers, such as Bay Secure Access Control, Funk, and Merit, and token providers like Security Dynamics, AXENT, Secure Computing, and LeeMah Datacom, so that you can easily incorporate the Extranet into your existing security infrastructure. It can use either its own internal lightweight directory access protocol (LDAP) server or an external LDAP server such as Netscape Directory Server to authenticate and differentiate among users.

Intrusion Detection System

Though many network security products like firewalls and authentication systems provide critical security, they offer limited visibility in the network data stream: Hackers could be using alternate means of access to your networks, such as dialing into a modem, dialing into someone's PC, or attacking from inside the organization. The NetRanger system from Cisco is the industry's first enterprise-scale, real-time network intrusion detection system to report and terminate unauthorized activity throughout a network. The NetRanger system can operate in both Internet and Intranet environments.

The NetRanger system has two components, the sensor and the director. The sensors, which are high-speed network appliances, analyze the content and context of individual packets to determine if traffic is authorized. If activity appears suspicious, suggesting a SATAN attack, a ping sweep, or the transmission of a secret research project code word, the sensors would then forward alarms to the director management console and remove the offender from the network. The director, a high-performance software-based management system, centrally monitors the activity of multiple sensors.

The proactive response functionality of the sensor allows users to automatically eliminate specific connections identified with unauthorized activity. The director remotely controls the configuration of the sensors from one centralized location. It can feed alarm information into a database archive to generate custom graphs and reports.

The NetRanger system reduces costs and ensures consistent security enforcement. In the NetRanger system:

- Real-time intrusion detection is transparent to legitimate traffic and network usage.

- Real-time response to unauthorized activity blocks offenders from accessing the network or terminates the offending sessions.

- A comprehensive attack signature list detects a wide range of attacks and can detect content and context-based attacks.

Locking Down Computers

Steel Security Cables

In order to stop someone from physically taking your computer, you need to lock it down. Steel security cables like those from Computer Security Products (*www.computersecurity.com*) are an easy way to deter hardware theft (see Figure 3.14). The company's PC Security Kits come with a hex fastener to protect internal components like RAM from theft. The disc fasteners attach to your computer. A cable can be secured to any immovable object.

FIGURE 3.14: PC Security Kits

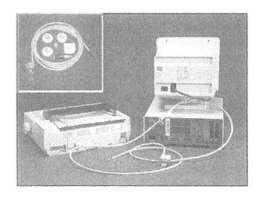

Source: Computer Security Products Inc.

Universal Drive Lock

In order to stop unauthorized users from transferring a virus by floppy disk, you have to secure the floppy drive on your computer. Universal Drive Lock from Innovative Security Products, (*www.wesecure.com*) provider of security devices for computers and office equipment, will lock up your external or internal drives, including nearly all floppy (see Figure 3.15), CD-ROM, Syquest, Iomega, tape back-up, Mac floppy with flat bezels, and notebook/laptop drives. Universal Drive Lock lets you leave a diskette or CD in the drive while using the lock.

FIGURE 3.15: Universal Drive Lock

Source: Innovative Security Products

Universal Drive Lock prevents:

- Introduction of an external virus to your computer and network
- Removal of sensitive files by unauthorized individuals
- Introduction of unauthorized software to PCs and networks

The Ultimate Security Kit

The Ultimate Security Kit (see Figure 3.16) from Innovative Security Products will both lock down a computer and sound an alarm. The kit will protect your PC or Mac with a 100+ decibel alarm if the unit is tampered with or the cable is cut. Two steel lock-down plates and a strong liquid adhesive offer up to 1,000 lbs. of holding strength.

The Ultimate Security Kit prevents:

- Theft of the monitor
- Theft of internal components such as the CPU
- Theft of the keyboard
- Theft of the printer or other peripheral

FIGURE 3.16: The Ultimate Security Kit

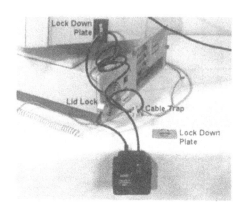

Source: Innovative Security Products

Laptop Security

Computer theft is second only to auto theft: In 1995 there were 208,000 notebook computers stolen in the U.S.; the losses in hardware, software, and data amounted to approximately $2 billion. Since laptops are becoming lighter and smaller, thieves have a greater chance to abscond with one within a few seconds. The data stored on a laptop can be more valuable than the laptop itself, especially if you are the target of industrial espionage.

Here are some ways to help keep your laptop secure:

- Keep good records. Serial numbers and a detailed description will help the police trace a stolen laptop and help you make an insurance claim.

- Using an etching tool, mark your name and phone number on your laptop.

- Never leave a laptop in a hotel room unattended. If the hotel has a safe, keep it there.

- Buy separate insurance if your business or home insurance does not cover your laptop.

• Keep your laptop in an ambiguous carrying case that looks like a traditional briefcase or any piece of carry-on luggage.

Security Devices

One preventive measure is a security cable. Master Lock and Kensington (*www.kensington.com*) have jointly developed the Universal Notebook Security Cable (see Figure 3.17), a simple system for quick and easy installation. The lock fits into your computer's built-in security slot, a feature developed by Kensington that is now an industry standard.

FIGURE 3.17: Kensington Universal Notebook Security Cable Kit

Source: Computer Security Products Inc.

To secure your portable computer, insert the lock into the built-in slot in your computer and wrap the cable around an immovable object like a table or desk. If no slot is available, the Security Slot Adapter Kit can be installed to secure the device.

Computer Security Products, Inc., has a product, CompuTrace Theft Recovery Software, to recover stolen laptops. CompuTrace, which works with any PC equipped with a modem, silently and periodically calls the CompuTrace Monitoring Center. The software is loaded onto the hard disk with a leading-edge stealth technology that hides from detection even by anti-virus software. Once activated, CompuTrace will make regular calls to a toll-free tracking line, logging and archiving every call for analysis.

CompuTrace is scheduled to call its toll-free tracking line every five to seven days. It will detect when the modem is connected and not in use before calling. When it initiates a call, CompuTrace disables the modem speaker. With each call, the computer's serial number and originating telephone number are logged. If the laptop has been reported stolen, CompuTrace will use its theft recovery procedure to locate it. The Theft Recovery Team coordinates the recovery of the stolen computer with local law enforcement.

Since CompuTrace does not appear in any directory, it is virtually impossible to remove. It cannot be erased off the hard disk by deleting files, formatting the hard disk, or even partitioning the hard disk.

CompuTrace:

- Reduces losses due to computer theft.
- Can be incorporated into a theft deterrent program to reduce losses.
- Makes it easy to manage your company's computer assets.
- Is undetectable, for maximum effectiveness.
- Is fully automated and maintenance-free.
- Is compatible with all phone systems and popular security software products.

Summary

Hardware security is more than locking the door to the computer room. Companies are using the Internet, Intranets, and Extranets to exchange information. Their employees use laptops wherever they go, carrying with them proprietary information. Hardware devices such as computer locks and smart cards help companies protect this information. Securing the organization's perimeter with alarms, surveillance cameras, and security guards make it transparent to intruders that security is enforced. Consider all possible security breaches and implement a security solution that encompasses them all.

With any security issue, the battle is ongoing. You will constantly need newer tools and technologies to keep one step ahead of all intruders.

References

Backman, Dan, "Smartcards: The Intelligent Way to Security," *Network Computing Online* (May 15, 1999). (*www.nwc.com/909/909 ws/2.html*).

Garfinkel, Simson, & Spafford, Gene, Practical UNIX & Internet Security (O'Reilly & Associates, 1966).

Harrison, Ann, "Tokens: Not Just for Security Any More," *ComputerWorld* (Mar. 22, 1999), p. 64.

Innovative Security Products, available on the World Wide Web at *www.wesecure.com*, 1998.

An Introduction to Computer Security: The NIST Handbook, Special Publication 800-12, (Feb. 7, 1996). (*www.csrc.ncsl.nist.gov/nist pubs/800-12*).

McCooey, Eileen, "Security Becomes a Priority," *Windows Magazine* (Jan. 1, 1999), p. 50.

NIST Computer Security Handbook of Cryptography, available at *http://security.isu.edu/isl/hk_crypt.html*.

Pasmore, Frank, "Weaving a Security Web," *Information Security Magazine*, available at *www.infosecuritymag.com*, April 1998.

Yasin, Rutrell, "Better Snapshots of Enterprise Security," *InternetWeek* (Feb. 22, 1999), p. 23.

Chapter 4*
Software Security

Vital information needs to flow freely from both inside and outside the company. But vital information is often both sensitive and confidential. It must be safeguarded.

Security Breaches

Security breaches are up in every category, says a 1998 *Information Security* industry study. The study surveyed 1,050 readers who worked in computer/data processing, education, finance/insurance, government, the law, manufacturing, health care, or the military.

Three out of four organizations experienced a virus in 1998, up from 68 percent in 1997. Employee access abuses are the second most common type of breach after viruses (Figure 4.1). Disgruntled employees can create havoc for companies with sensitive information. Nearly one in five companies experienced a dramatic increase in leakages of proprietary information, *Information Security* said.

Although three out of four organizations experienced a virus last year, nine out of ten have a virus protection product in place (Table 4.1). With the increased growth in the Internet, Internet security is another major problem your company has to deal with, yet as Table 4.1 shows, only six out of ten organizations have in place Internet/Intranet/Web security. That is likely to change as more organizations have a Web presence and engage in e-commerce. Table 4.2 shows the products and services organizations plan to purchase in the near future.

---

*This chapter was coauthored by Robert Fonfeder, Ph.D., CPA, professor in the School of Business at Hofstra University.

FIGURE 4.1: Industry Breaches; Types of Breaches Experienced

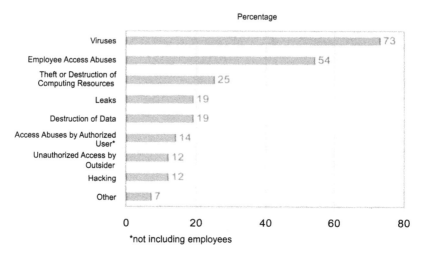

31% of those suffering a breach said they suffered a business-operations setback, while 18% said they suffered a financial loss.

Source: Information Security

TABLE 4.1: Top 10 Information Security Products and Services Now In Use

Virus protection	91%
Backup storage	90%
Access controls	85%
Physical security	80%
Firewalls	74%
Client/server security	73%
LAN/WAN security	67%
Disaster-recovery services	61%
E-mail security	61%
Internet/Intranet/Web security	60%

Source: Information Security

TABLE 4.2: Top 10 Products and Services Organizations Plan to Buy
in the "Near Future"

Encryption	32%
Training/education	28%
Virtual private networks (VPN)	27%
Internet/Intranet/Web security	27%
Firewalls	26%
E-mail security	25%
Smart cards	21%
Disaster recovery services	21%
Network/communications security	18%
Client/server security	18%

Source: Information Security

Malicious Codes

IT managers need to address a variety of malicious codes. The best
known are viruses, but others are worms, Trojan horses, droppers, and
bombs.

Worms

A worm is a program on either a non-networked or networked computer
that replicates itself but does not infect other programs. In a network setting a worm copies itself to and from floppy disks or across network connections. In a non-networked computer it can copy itself to different locations on hard disks. In either case, worms often steal and vandalize computer data.

Trojan Horses

A Trojan horse is a bad program hidden inside a seemingly harmless program. When that program is run, the Trojan horse launches in order to
perform an unexpected task. Trojan horses do not replicate themselves,
but they can steal passwords, delete data, format hard drives, or cause
other problems.

Droppers

A dropper is a program designed to avoid anti-virus detection, usually by encryption that prevents anti-virus software from noticing it. Typical functions of droppers include transport and installation of viruses. They wait on the system for a specific event, at which point they infect the system with the virus they contain.

Bombs

A bomb is a malicious script or scheduling program that activates when a specific event occurs. Some bombs activate at a specific time, typically using the system clock. A bomb could be programmed, for instance, to erase all DOC files from your hard disk on New Year's Eve, or to pop up a message on a famous person's birthday. Another bomb might wait for the twentieth time a program is launched and then erase the program's template files.

Viruses

A computer virus is a program that replicates and spreads by attaching itself to other programs. When the infected program is run, the virus executes an event, which can be:

- *Benign*, displaying a message on a certain date
- *Annoying*, slowing performance or altering the screen display
- *Catastrophic*, erasing files, destroying data, or crashing systems

Viruses can be spread through droppers and use the worm idea to replicate themselves. They can act as Trojan horses by attaching themselves to an existing program, hiding inside the program, launching when the program launches, and committing unwanted acts.

The different types of viruses include:

- *Boot sector viruses*, infectors residing on a hard disk that are read and executed by the computer at boot time. Boot sector viruses can infect either the DOS boot sector or the master boot record, being loaded into memory during the boot process.
- *File infectors* are parasitic viruses that attach themselves to executable files. These viruses wait in memory for you to run another program. They replicate simply through the use of the computer.

- *Macro viruses* affect programs such as Microsoft Office that ship with programs built-in. When a document or template containing the macro virus is opened, the virus does its damage. These viruses are also programmed to copy themselves into other documents to continually spread.

- *Multipartite viruses* combine boot sector with file infections.

- *Stealth viruses* mislead anti-virus software into acting as if nothing is wrong. They retain information about the files they have infected, wait in memory, and intercept anti-virus programs looking for altered files, giving the anti-virus programs the old information rather than the new.

- *Polymorphic viruses* alter themselves when they replicate so that anti-virus software looking for specific patterns will not find them all. Those viruses that survive can continue replicating.

- *Future new viruses* are likely to be numerous and unpredictable.

How Viruses Spread

Viruses come from a variety of sources, and because they can attach themselves to legitimate software, they can pass many security defenses. In a 1991 study of major U.S. and Canadian computer users by Dataquest, the market research firm for the National Computer Security Association, viruses were shown to spread from the following sources:

- 87% of users blamed an infected diskette.

- 43% of the diskettes responsible for introducing a virus into a corporate computing environment were brought from home.

- 6% of infected diskettes were demo disks, diagnostic disks used by service technicians, or shrink-wrapped software disks.

- 71% of infections occurred in a networked environment, making rapid spread of viruses a serious risk.

- 7% had come from software downloaded from an electronic bulletin board service.

Viruses can be downloaded from trial programs, a macro from a specific program, or an attachment to an e-mail message. A virus delivered as an e-mail attachment, however, does nothing until you double-click on the attachment. One way to protect yourself from this virus is never to open attachments that are executable files or data files for programs.

Symptoms of Viruses

Most common viruses give off no symptoms of infection; anti-virus tools are necessary to identify and eradicate them. However, the many viruses that are flawed do provide some tip-offs to their presence. Symantec, maker of Norton anti-virus software, (*www.symantec.com/avcenter/security/index.html*) suggests that you watch for:

- Changes in the length of programs
- Changes in the file date or time stamp
- Longer program load times
- Slower system operation
- Reduced memory or disk space
- Bad sectors on your floppy
- Unusual error messages
- Unusual screen activity
- Failed program execution
- Failed system boot-ups when booting or accidentally booting from the A: drive
- Unexpected writes to a drive

Anti-Virus Software

Norton Anti-Virus

To fully protect your corporate network from viruses, you will need to install anti-virus software. Norton AntiVirus software from Symantec is a good choice for Windows workstations and servers. Features in version 5.0 let you quarantine infected files and automatically protect you against not only viruses but also malicious ActiveX and Java applets. Norton AntiVirus runs in the background.

Some key features of Norton AntiVirus 5.0 are:

- *Quarantine:* It isolates infected files in a safe corner of your computer until you can repair the damage.

- *Scan and deliver:* It easily sends quarantined or other suspicious files to Symantec for evaluation and repair.

- *LiveUpDate:* automatically retrieves new virus definitions from Symantec as often as once a week.

- *Protection against malicious codes:* detects and removes dangerous forms of ActiveX code, Java applets, and Trojan horses.

- *24-hour protection:* runs constantly in the background.

Dr. Solomon's Anti-Virus Deluxe

Another good anti-virus software product is Dr. Solomon's Anti-Virus Deluxe from McAfee. Dr. Solomon's WinGuard scanner and NetGuard provide 24-hour virus protection from Internet downloads, shared files, e-mail, floppies, and hard disks. The program detects viruses in compressed and archives files. It also includes an SOS disk that lets you boot from a clean diskette, even if your operating system will not load. With the SOS disk you can have a virus-free system before you install Dr. Solomon's anti-virus software. Dr. Solomon provides free automatic update to the most current version of the software and protection updates to the hundreds of new viruses that appear each month.

Total Virus Defense

With over 22,000 existing viruses and over 300 new ones being created each month, protecting a diverse network from them is no easy task. Total Virus Defense 4.0 is a complete virus security solution from Network Associates, a provider of enterprise anti-virus solutions, and Dr. Solomon, a company in detection and cleaning technology. Total Virus Defense keeps your network protected enterprise-wide, at the desktop, file and groupware servers, and the Internet.

Total Virus Defense ensures protection of your PC from all sources of viruses, including floppy disks, Internet downloads, e-mail attachments, networks, shared files, CD-ROM, online services, and even most popular compressed file types. The total Virus Defense Suite includes:

- *VirusScan:* detects and removes viruses from desktop clients.

- *NetShield:* detects virus-infected files transmitted to and from the server to prevent the spread of viruses throughout the network.

- *GroupShield:* scans groupware environments (Lotus Notes or Microsoft Exchange) to stop viruses before they're distributed.

- *WebShield:* scans all inbound and outbound e-mail passing through an SMTP e-mail gateway, automatically cleans or quarantines files, and sends alerts to system administrators.

The Total Virus Defense AutoUpdate feature works through scheduled downloads from a central server. AutoImmune lets your company automatically detect, remove, and create a cure for previously unknown viruses. Anti-Virus Informant allows network administrators to proactively monitor virus defense.

Firewalls

A firewall is a system or group of systems that enforces an access control policy between two networks. It's a security enforcement point that separates a trusted network from an untrusted one, such as the Internet (see Figure 4.2). It screens all connections between networks, determining which traffic should be allowed and which should not. The security administrator determines in advance how the firewall should set the rules to separate networks.

FIGURE 4.2: Firewall

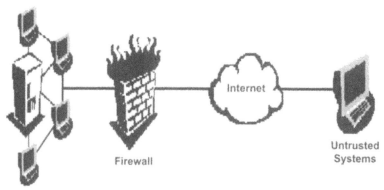

Source: Network Associates, 1999

Firewalls commonly:

- Secure network access with a perimeter defense.
- Control all connections into and out of the network.
- Filter data according to defined rules.
- Authenticate users and applications before permitting them to access internal resources.
- Log activities for security auditing purposes.
- Actively notify the appropriate people when suspicious events occur.

Firewalls not only protect the internal corporate network from the public Internet, they can separate individual departments from the rest of the network. With internal firewalls, security administrators can apply different access control rules across a wide variety of working groups and network subnets, thus providing a layer of protection against internal breaches. For example, a firewall can be placed in front of the Human Resources department to deter access by other departments to sensitive personnel data.

When you connect to the Internet, you're putting three things at risk:

- Your data—the information you keep on the computers
- Your resources—the computers themselves
- Your reputation—which can be affected by others using your identity

The Internet presents marvelous opportunities for people to exchange ideas and information. At the same time, the risks are out there. A firewall is the most effective way to connect to the Internet and still protect your network (Chapman, 1995), though building a firewall requires significant expense and effort, and the restrictions it places on insiders can be a major annoyance.

Once in place, firewalls do offer significant benefits. They allow you to:

- Focus your security decisions.
- Enforce security policy.
- Log Internet activity efficiently.
- Limit your exposure.

Firewalls offer excellent protection against network threats, but they are not a complete security solution (Chapman, 1995). Certain threats outside the control of the firewall need to be addressed by other means. For example, a firewall works well in protecting your network from outsiders but not from someone on your side of the firewall—58% of security threats originate from employees, contractors, consultants, and other internal users (see Figure 4.3). Firewalls:

- Do not protect you against malicious insiders.
- Do not protect you against connections that do not go through it.
- Do not protect against completely new threats.
- Do not protect against viruses.

FIGURE 4.3: Security Breaches

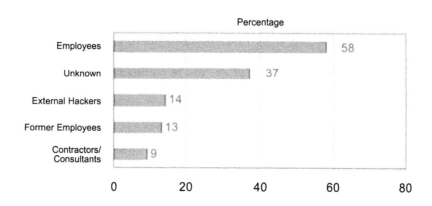

Source: Information Week/PriceWaterhouse Coopers, 1998

Packet Filter Firewalls

Most organizations that want a high-performance yet easy-to-configure firewall will implement packet filter firewalls. In packet filtering the firewall checks each incoming or outgoing IP packet header against a table of access control rules. If the address and port information are acceptable, the packet proceeds through the firewall directly to its destination. If not, the packet is dropped at the firewall. Elaborate rules can be developed to allow or disallow certain packets.

Packet-filtering firewalls are fast because they operate at the network layer and make only cursory checks into the validity of a given connection (see Figure 4.4). Unfortunately, they have low security and no effect on application vulnerabilities. Once a connection has been approved by the firewall, the outside source can connect directly through to the target destination, potentially exposing the internal network to attack by direct connection with untrusted external sources.

FIGURE 4.4: Packet Filter Firewall

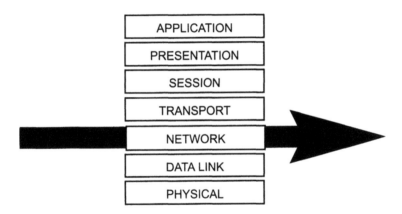

Source: Network Associates White Paper, 1999

Application Proxy Firewall

Government agencies such as DARPA (Defense Advanced Research Projects Agency) and the U.S. Department of Defense started looking for a better approach to firewall security. The application proxy firewall that resulted provides full application-level awareness of attempted connections by examining everything at the highest layer of the protocol stack (Figure 4.5).

An application proxy firewall can easily see the granular details of each attempted connection up front and implement security policies accordingly (Gauntlet, NAI, 1999). The built-in proxy function terminates the client connection at the firewall and initiates a new connection to the internal protected network, thus preventing any direct contact between trusted and untrusted systems. A proxy firewall makes it more difficult for hackers on the outside to exploit vulnerabilities on systems inside the firewall.

FIGURE 4.5: Application Proxy Firewall

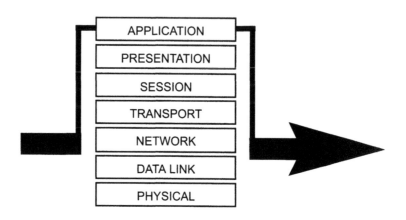

Source: Network Associates White Paper, 1999

Proxy Server

Spoofing is a way of using a valid internal IP address to pretend that the foreign system is inside your secure walls. Packet filtering alone is not enough to stop a break-in attempt because it does not prevent spoofing. As a result, many companies have migrated to proxy server firewalls. The proxy server resides between a client application such as a Web browser and a real server. It allows internal clients to access the Internet from behind a firewall, intercepting all requests from clients within the firewall and forwarding them to the real server.

However, there is a downside to proxy servers: The overhead required to run an application proxy is considerably higher than a packet filter, which significantly slows network traffic.

Hybrid Firewalls

In 1998 a few vendors like Check Point and Network Associates addressed this problem by designing "hybrid" firewalls. As the name suggests, hybrid firewalls combine the best of both worlds: the speed of a packet filter and the stringent security features of an application proxy (Foote, 1999). Hybrid firewalls use packet filtering during peak hours when there is a lot of network traffic, but if the firewall perceives a threat, the application proxies take control. Once a connection has been established through a proxy, all subsequent traffic is filtered, thereby balancing speed with security.

A Complete Firewall Security System

The Internet can link a company with customers, remote employees, suppliers, and business partners at a fraction of the cost of other linkages. To remain competitive means that private networks must be able to extend to the outside world.

With the increasingly sophisticated security threats from new technologies, having stand-alone firewalls to protect a network is not enough. Integrated network security that actively communicates with other security tools and responds to new attacks by modifying security measures accordingly is needed (see Figure 4.6). The role of the firewall has to evolve from a stand-alone system enforcing access rules into a distributed system integrating components throughout the network.

FIGURE 4.6: Distributed Firewall System

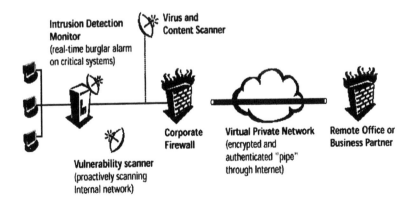

Source: Network Associates

A complete security system must have the following components:

- Firewalls that guard against unauthorized entry from outsiders or individual departments
- Vulnerability scanners that proactively scan the internal network for potential security holes or weaknesses
- Intrusion detection monitors that watch internal network traffic and servers for signs of attack
- Virus and content scanners searching for malicious code such as viruses, Trojan horses, or hostile Java and ActiveX applets
- A central event manager that meaningfully integrates the distributed security components (all monitors, sensors, and scanners)

Thus companies cannot rely on passive firewalls that guard only the front entrance. Firewalls have to work with other security components to actively respond to changing threats. Network Associates now has an active firewall system called the Gauntlet Active Firewall (see Figure 4.7) that combines proactive vulnerability scanning, real-time intrusion detection monitoring, anti-virus scanning, and virtual private networking into a single active system.

FIGURE 4.7: The Active Firewall

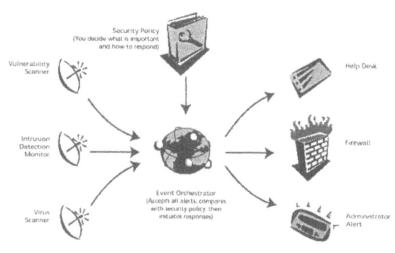

Source: Network Associates

This scenario can demonstrate how the Gauntlet Active Firewall works: Every morning at 2:00 a.m. the vulnerability scanner runs through a series of routine vulnerability tests. During one of these, it discovers that an employee has set her PC up as an insecure FTP server that exposes data on the private network to attack. The scanner forwards this information to the Event Orchestrator so that it can check the customer's security policy to determine the appropriate course of action.

The Event Orchestrator then instructs the firewall to shut down the FTP server until the IT staff arrives the following morning. The Event Orchestrator can also send a trouble ticket describing the problem to the help desk. When in the morning the user calls the help desk because her FTP service is not working, the IT staff, already aware of that, can then advise her of the security risks her actions have created.

Encryption

Encryption is the translation of data into a secret code, a method of scrambling information so that only the intended receiver can use it. It uses algorithms to mathematically combine "keys" with plain text to form encrypted or cipher text. It's the most effective security device because you must have a specific key to unlock the data.

Any digital data can be encrypted, including e-mail messages, telephone calls, movies, pictures, and computer files. Today there are both hardware devices and software packages available for encrypting data.

There are two main types of encryption: *symmetric* (secret key) encryption and *asymmetric* (public key) encryption. Secret key encryption uses one key. Public key encryption uses a pair of keys called public and private keys.

Secret Key Encryption

Before the creation of the public/private key method, a technology called symmetric cryptography was used. Here the sender uses the secret key (a large binary number) algorithm to mathematically encrypt the communication and the recipient uses the same key to decrypt it. Secret key encryption is relatively fast and small. It's often generated in Web browsers each time they open a secure transaction. Using secret key cryptography, it's safe to send encrypted messages without fear of interception because it's not likely that the message can be deciphered (see Figure 4.8).

FIGURE 4.8: Symmetric Keys

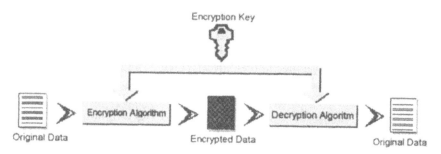

Source: Symantec Corporation

The problem with this method, however, is figuring out how to deliver the secret key to the recipient either through another secure transmission channel or in person. If the secret key is intercepted, all communications are compromised. Moreover, the infrastructure is impractical for a large number of people. If you have a large organization, you may need thousands (if not millions) of secret keys. In addition, secret key cryptography assumes that the parties who share a key will not disclose or modify the key.

The method does not ensure the authenticity of the sending party. If Bob receives an encrypted message, he has no way of proving who sent it.

The best-known secret-key system is the Data Encryption Standard (DES) published by the National Institute of Standards and Technology as Federal Information Processing Standards (FIPS) 46-2. NIST is an agency of the U.S. Department of Commerce's Technology Administration. FIPS is the official series of publications relating to standards and guidelines mandated by the Secretary of Commerce.

Since 1977 DES has been the federal government's standard method for encrypting sensitive information. The algorithm standard has, moreover, evolved from solely a U.S. government algorithm into one that is used globally by the commercial sector. It's the most widely accepted, publicly available cryptographic system today.

Public Key Cryptography

A major advance occurred with the invention of public key cryptography. Public key (asymmetric) cryptography uses a "public" key and a "private" key that are mathematically tied together. Using this method a message is encrypted with a public key, and the private key is used to decrypt the same message (see Figure 4.9). The public key may be distributed to the world because it is used only for encrypting. Its owner must keep the private key confidential. The encrypted message can only be decrypted with its matching private key. This protocol is used with Secure Sockets Layers (SST) technology, which is the standard protocol for secure Web-based communications.

FIGURE 4.9: Public/Private Keys

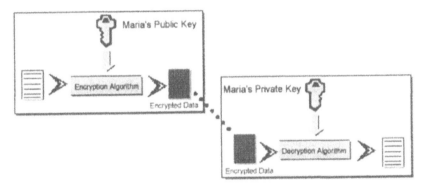

Source: Symantec Corporation

Public key technology is a breakthrough because it solves the key management problem associated with symmetric key encryption in large organizations. It also reduces the possibility of key compromise during delivery.

Before the invention of public key cryptography, it was virtually impossible to provide key management to large-scale networks. The number of keys required to secure communications among those users increased substantially as the number of users grew. For example, a network of 100 users would require almost 5,000 keys if it used only secret key cryptography. Doubling the network to 200 users increases the number of keys needed to almost 20,000.

Public key encryption, however, is bulky and slow. It doesn't easily encrypt a file once for a number of different people. Users who lose their keys will not be able to decrypt files encrypted with those keys. It also doesn't guarantee that John's public key is not someone else pretending to be John. As a result, most encryption systems use both types of encryption.

Combination Encryption

Public/private key pairs are very long and time-consuming. To speed the process and make it more secure, both methods—symmetric and public key encryption—are used together. In the scenario shown in Figure 4.10, Bill has a message that he wants to send to Maria. Bill sues a symmetric key to encrypt the document and then encrypts the symmetric key using Maria's public key.

FIGURE 4.10: Encrypt with Symmetric and Public Keys

Bill's Computer

Bill uses a symmetric key to encrypt a document.

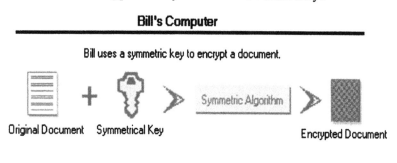

Original Document   Symmetrical Key   Encrypted Document

Then he encrypts the symmetric key using Maria's public key.

Symmetrical Key   Maria's Public Key   Encrypted Symmetric Key

Source: Symantec Corporation

When Maria receives the encrypted message from Bill, she uses her private key to decrypt the symmetrical key (see Figure 4.11). Then Maria uses the symmetric key to decrypt the message.

FIGURE 4.11: Decrypt Using Private and Symmetric Keys

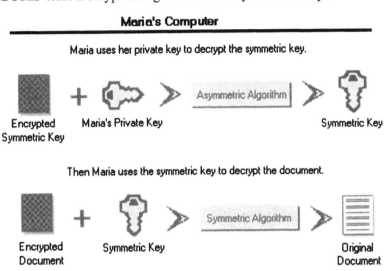

Source: Symantec Corporation

Encryption in On-line Trading

One of the major uses of public/private key technology is in on-line trading where security is a major concern for both investors and brokers. The top five on-line brokers—E*Trade, DLJdirect, Discover Brokerage, Waterhouse, and Datek—ensure the security of customer's account information by using encryption to safeguard against hackers intercepting a customer's user ID and password and posing as the actual customer.

The on-line brokerage firm keeps one key—the private key (Figure 4.12). It makes the other key -- the public key—available to customers. Anyone who finds the public key can use it only to send the firm a private message (see Figure 4.13). It cannot be used to decrypt messages sent to the firm or to imitate the firm. Therefore, the firm can send the public key to customers using e-mail or it can even post the key on its Web site.

FIGURE 4.12: Public and Private Keys

Source: VeriSign Inc.

FIGURE 4.13: Encrypt and Decrypt

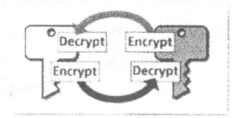

Source: VeriSign Inc.

In public/private key encryption, the customer's computer verifies the broker's server by checking the broker's digital signature and comparing it against the signature on record in a digital certificate. Digital certificates are sent by a third-party registrar like VeriSign Inc. Then the customer's and broker's computers use a session key. The session key (Figure 4.14) is used to encrypt all the data transferred during the session. The key ranges in length from 40 to 128 bits, depending on the level of security supported by the Web browsers of both parties. This complicated conversion makes an intercepted message virtually impossible to decode. Even if a hacker happens to access a customer's account, funds can be transferred only to a bank account the customer has previously specified.

FIGURE 4.14: Session Key Used to Place an Order

Source: VeriSign Inc.

FIGURE 4.15: Each Transaction Uses a Session Key

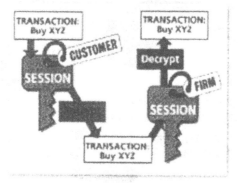

Source: VeriSign Inc.

Each transaction uses a session key (Figure 4.15). When a customer buys, the transaction gets encrypted using the session key. When the firm receives the order, the firm uses its session key to decrypt it. This process is not contingent on the next transaction. When a customer buys again, a new session key is created. Even if a hacker decodes one transaction, the next will be entirely different.

Digital Signatures

Authentication generally has two components, one to prove that the information came from a specific user and the second to prove that the information has not been altered. Authentication is possible through the use of a digital signature, a technique that uses public key encryption to "sign" electronic documents.

Digital signature is a code that can be attached to an electronically transmitted message that uniquely identifies the sender. Like a written signature, the purpose of a digital signature is to guarantee that the individual sending the message really is who he or she claims to be. Digital signatures not only allow for strong authentication and data integrity but also non-repudiation: When participants transact business electronically using digital signatures, they cannot deny the transaction.

Digital signature schemes have two steps:

1. Generating a message digest ("hash") of the message

2. Generating the signature by combining the message digest with the user's secret key

Adding a signature to a message validates the integrity of the message. Digital signature confirms that the message has not been altered since you signed it because any changes to the message after you sign will invalidate the signature.

All the trust in the signature, however, is tied to whether or not you can trust the signer's public key. If you cannot verify that the public key belongs to the specific person, corporation, or authorized agent, then digital signatures can be forged.

Public Key Infrastructure

Since key management and digital signatures are based on public key technologies, good information security requires a public key infrastructure (PKI). PKI is a system of digital certificates, certificate authorities, and other registration authorities that authenticate the validity of each party to an Internet transaction. There is no single PKI, or even a single agreed standard for setting up a PKI. Implementing public key encryption, digital signature, and other security services on a broad scale will require many certificate authorities.

Entrust/PKI. Entrust Technologies, Inc., provides the Entrust/PKI to allow people to encrypt, digitally sign, and authenticate electronic transactions across all applications. Entrust/PKI is a managed PKI. In a managed PKI, the users in one certificate authority (CA) can communicate securely with users from another CA. A managed PKI is thus a method for maintaining trustworthy electronic relationships between CAs. Entrust/PKI policy management provides security, flexibility, and ease of use through a wide range of network policy options.

Kerberos. Kerberos is an authentication system created at the Massachusetts Institute of Technology (MIT) as a solution to network security problems carried by insiders. Designed to enable two parties to exchange private information across an insecure network connection, it works by assigning a unique key, called a ticket, to each user that logs on to the network. The ticket is then embedded in messages to identify the sender of the message. Kerberos provides the tools of authentication and strong cryptography to help secure information systems across your enterprise.

Pretty Good Privacy. Pretty Good Privacy (PGP) is a technique for encrypting messages developed by Philip Zimmerman. PGP is one of the most common ways to protect messages on the Internet because it is effective, easy to use—and free. PGP is based on the public-key method. To encrypt a message using PGP, you need the PGP encryption package, which is available from a number of sources, including MIT.

PGP Enterprise Security Suite, with applications for Win32, Mac, and UNIX environments, is a complete e-mail, file, disk, and network security product from Network Associates. PGP users can send strongly encrypted files to non-PGP users with self-decrypting files. The Suite integrates security and authentication for e-mail, files, and disks by integrating:

- *PGP VPN Client*, which uses either PGP or X.509-based certificates for secure VPN and remote Internet access to your network

- *PGP Desktop Security*, which secures e-mail and files by encrypting and digitally signing for data protection and authentication

- *Certificate Server*, through which organizations can create and manage a unified public-key infrastructure that enables confidential communications across a corporate Intranet or Extranet or the public Internet

- *Policy Management Agent*, which enforces corporate security policies for e-mail communications across internal and external networks

- *PGP Software Developers Toolkit*, which can incorporate trusted and peer-reviewed PGP cryptographic capabilities into new and existing applications

With PGP Enterprise Security Suite, e-mails, files, and disks can be secured and authenticated as quickly as doing a "save." The Suite also supports current standards such as IPSec and X.509, the most widely used standard for defining digital certificates.

The Orange Book

Trusted Computer System Evaluation Criteria, better known as the Orange Book, is a U.S. government publication that standardizes security system requirements. It defines four broad categories of security for host-based environments:

- Minimal security (least)
- Discretionary protection
- Mandatory protection
- Verified protection (most)

The objectives of the Orange Book are to:

1. Provide a way of assessing the level to which you can trust a given computer system.
2. Provide guidelines to manufacturers as to what to build into their systems to satisfy various security needs.
3. Serve as a basis for specifying security requirements so you can purchase a coordinated security system.

In today's complex business environments, though, the Orange Book's security classifications are somewhat limited (Innovative Security Products, 1998).

Security in a Distributed Network

In the past IT managers planning to secure their companies' applications and systems had to use a variety of tools to gather all the reports. AXENT Technologies, Inc. (*www.axent.com*) has alleviated this by creating a product called Enterprise Security Manager 5.0 (ESM). ESM allows administrators to check, manage, and enforce security policies from a central console, offloading repetitive tasks associated with managing security policy from human staff members to computers.

ESM is based on manager/agent architecture. Software agents residing in servers and workstations gather pertinent data and send them to the ESM console. A single console can collect data from and manage up to 10,000 software agents. ESM console and advanced reporting features provide a snapshot of security levels across the enterprise in a single graph (Yasin, 1999). Only data that is absolutely necessary gets sent between agents and managers, using less networking bandwidth for security checks. All agents can be run manually on a schedule, depending on what you need to proactively manage your corporate computing environment.

ESM offers the following benefits:

- *Consistency across platforms:* It evaluates all systems based on a standard security policy.
- *Broad platform support:* It supports over 35 operating systems, including Windows NT, UNIX, NetWare, and Open VMS.
- *Dynamic configuration:* It allows you to customize policies to meet the needs of your unique environment.
- *Integrated reporting capabilities:* It allows you to go from enterprise-wide reporting to individual security settings with just a few clicks of the mouse.
- *Intuitive graphical user interface (GUI):* The interface for configuring, managing, and reporting on security policies across your enterprise is easy to use.
- *Fast correction of security problems:* You can quickly correct faulty security settings and update groups of systems to security settings mandated in the security policy.
- *Compatibility with existing systems:* It integrates easily with existing security applications and processes.
- *Manager/agent architecture:* ESM's manager and agents can be different systems, allowing you to leverage your existing security systems.
- *Hierarchical approach:* It's scalable to your enterprise network.

Total Network Security

For IT managers looking for a one-stop network security solution, IBM's Integrated Security Solutions enables companies to turn to a single vendor for all security software, hardware, and services needed when moving their business to the Internet. The system has three parts:

- *IBM SecureWay FirstSecure* integrates security for Web-based systems with legacy-based systems

- *Tivoli Availability* provides uninterrupted network services.

- *Tivoli Administration* provides centralized, consistent ways to manage a secure network.

The Internet Security Market

According to a study released March 30, 1999, by International Data Corp. (IDC), the worldwide market for Internet security software grew from $2 billion in 1997 to an estimated $3.1 billion in 1998. Security threats continue to increase as more companies provide access to the internal systems via the Internet for things like e-commerce, prompting many companies to increase spending on security software (Perez, 1999). Based on the IDC study of 300 companies with more than $100 million in annual revenues, the 1999 market for Internet security software is estimated at $4.2 billion worldwide, growing to $7.4 billion in 2002.

In general, the Internet software security market is expected to have a compound annual revenue growth rate of about 30% between now and 2002, IDC said. IDC reports that the top three segments of this market are likely to be:

- *Firewall*, the fastest-growing segment, with an estimated 40% compound annual growth

- *Anti-virus software*, likely to be the largest segment of the market in 2002, accounting for almost half of the worldwide revenues from Internet security software

- *Encryption software*, plus software authorization, authentication, and administration

Security Protocols

SSL

Secure Sockets Layer (SSL) is the Internet security protocol for point-to-point connections. With the growth of the Internet, many applications need to securely transmit data to remote applications and computers. SSL was designed to solve this problem. Many popular Web browsers like Netscape Communication and Internet Explorer use SSL to protect against eavesdropping, tampering, and forgery. In SSL, when clients and servers make connections, they authenticate each other. Once authenticated, a "secure pipe" is established and data can be securely exchanged (see Figure 4.16). SSL uses strong encryption technologies from RSA Data Security.

FIGURE 4.16: Secure Socket Layer

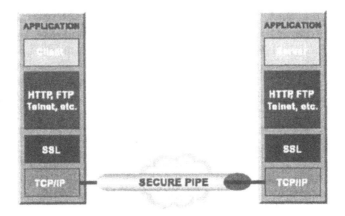

Source: RSA Data Security

Some practical applications of SSL are:

- *Client/server systems:* Securing database access
- *Financial:* Remote banking programs
- *Information systems:* Remote access and administration applications
- *Travel industry:* Create online reservation systems and secure information transfer

IPSec

Internet Protocol Security (IPSec), a set of protocols developed by the Internet Engineering Task Force (IETF) for encryption and authentication of TCP/IP traffic, is the leading standard for cryptographically based authentication, integrity, and privacy services.

At the IP layer, computers on a network communicate by routing datagram packets that contain data, destination addresses, source addresses, and other information. In a corporate LAN or the Internet, where packet datagrams are transmitted "as is," unencrypted, a malicious attacker could hijack, forge, or modify them. IPSec secures the network packets to create a secure network of computers over insecure channels. It enables users to communicate securely with a remote host over the Internet via VPNs. Where SSL authenticates and encrypts communications between clients and servers at the application layer, IPSec secures the underlying network layer.

Some practical applications of IPSec are:

- *VPN software and hardware:* Creating secure networks over insecure means of transmission such as the Internet
- *Remote access software and hardware:* Securing access to network resources
- *Firewall products:* Securing VPN tunneling to link business partners and members of the enterprise

S/MIME

Secure Multipurpose Internet Mail Extensions (S/MIME) is the electronic standard that protects messages from unauthorized interception and forgery. S/MIME uses public-key encryption technology to secure transmission, storage, authentication, and forwarding of secret data. Where SSL secures a connection between a client and a server over an insecure network, S/MIME is used to secure users, applications, and computers.

Some practical applications of S/MIME are:

- *Electronic data exchange (EDI):* digital signatures on contracts
- *Financial messaging:* store and transfer bank statements
- *Content delivery:* electronic bill payment
- *Health care:* secure patient records and health claims

Like SSL and IPSec, S/MIME is based on the RSA algorithm for digital signatures and digital envelopes (see Table 4.3).

TABLE 4.3: Security Protocols Overview

Protocol	Summary
SSL (Secure Socket Layer)	Allows a "secure pipe" between any two applications for transfer of data and mutual authentication
IPSec (IP Security Protocol)	Standard for cryptographically-based authentication, integrity, and confidentiality services at the IP datagram layer
S/MIME (Secure MIME)	Guarantees the secure transmission, storage, authentication, and forwarding of secret data at the application level

Source: RSA Data Security

VPNs

Virtual private networks (VPNs) allow communication between sites using a public network such as the Internet to go over an encrypted channel. Since network communication over the Internet is vulnerable to "snooping" (electronic eavesdropping), setting up a VPN guarantees private communication between two sites. VPNs also represent cost savings over true private networks such as leased line an frame relay because they reduce connectivity costs.

A successful VPN deployment is much more than simple data encryption. A complete VPN solution includes:

- *Security:* granular access control, user authentication, standards-based data encryption to guarantee the security of network connections, authenticity of users, and privacy and integrity of data communications

- *Traffic control:* band-width management, quality of service, and acceleration of data encryption/decryption to guarantee VPN reliability and performance

- *Enterprise management:* a comprehensive security policy that integrates enterprise-wide VPNs and centralized policy-based management

Remote Access Security Solution

The Internet has brought many corporations more flexibility in allowing their workers to telecommute or work in remote locations, but the corporations need to ensure that remote users have access to the resources they need without sacrificing corporate network security. They have to prevent unauthorized users from gaining access to the corporate network by impersonating legitimate users. AXENT Technologies, Inc., has a complete remote access security solution called Security Briefcase for Windows 95 and Windows NT. Security Briefcase provides a complete enterprise policy-based solution by protecting the local disk, preventing unauthorized users from accessing corporate information, and securing the session over the Internet (see Figure 4.17).

FIGURE 4.17: Security Briefcase

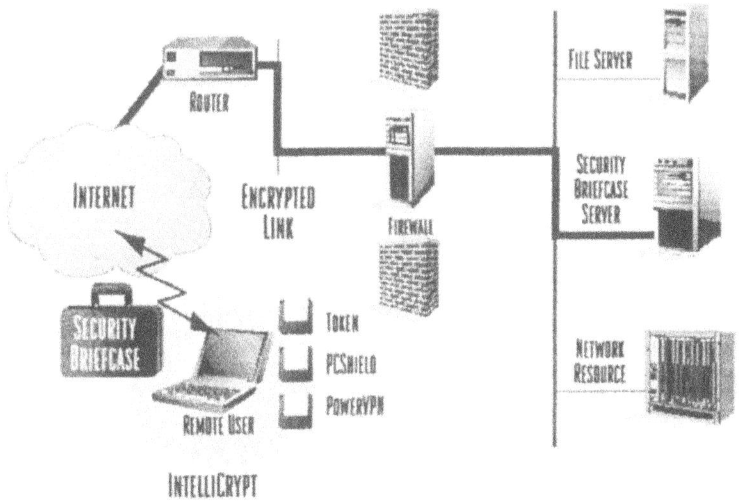

Source: AXENT Technologies Inc.

Defender

Passwords may be compromised with hacker tools such as password sniffers, network sniffers, and dictionary attacks. Once passwords are stolen, unauthorized users can easily access your files. Security Briefcase provides two-factor user authentication consisting of a token and a PIN.

Power VPN

VPNs encapsulate data packets, securing your Internet communications. The Power VPN feature of AXENT's Briefcase (see Figure 4.18), which does not require modification of your application software or the network, reduces your telecommunications costs by providing access directly to your VPN through any ISP, eliminating the need for maintaining costly toll-free numbers. Users dial into a local ISP and tunnel securely to the corporate network.

FIGURE 4.18: Comparison Between Firewall Only and PowerVPN

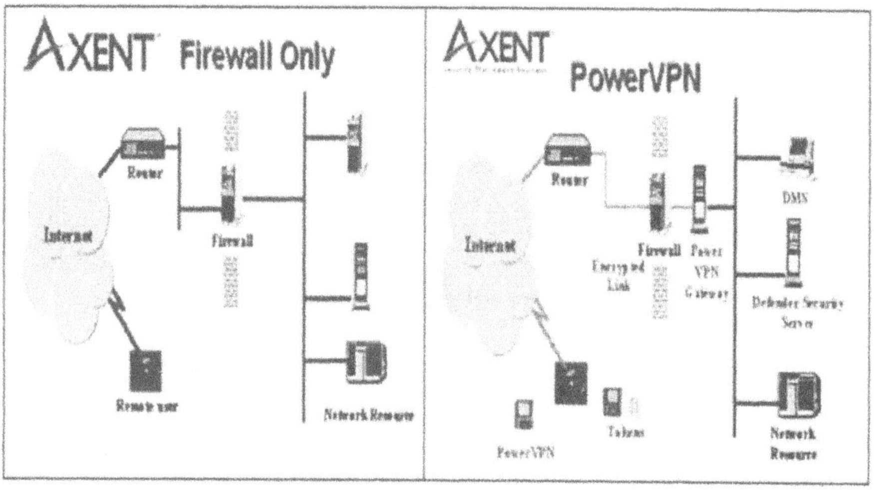

Source: AXENT Technologies Inc.

PowerVPN consists of a client that runs on a PC or laptop and a gateway behind the firewall (see Figure 4.18). The secure and authenticated connection is between the PC that uses the PowerVPN encryption session to connect to the Power VPN gateway at the corporate network. Unlike VPN from other firewall vendors, Power VPN operates independent of the firewall, making firewalls instantly compatible with PowerVPN. PowerVPN increases throughput by compressing the data before encrypting it.

PCShield

The PCShield feature of the Security Briefcase protects data on your PC from unauthorized users by providing automatic file encryption and decryption, and centralized key management, all in one product. PCShield provides centralized administration of PC and laptop security. A central database contains all user accounts, groups, file access control rules, and audit standards, making it possible to know which computers each user can access. This entire secure authentication is integrated into the product, making the process transparent to the Windows operating systems and applications.

PCShield automatically protects new files from unauthorized access. It secures files that are stored locally, on file servers, on floppy drives, or even transmitted across the network. PCShield adds an access control label to each protected file so that the protection stays with the file wherever it resides. It also encrypts data automatically. When a PC is left unattended or connected to the network, users must re-enter their passwords to regain access to the system. Information cannot be accessed on a protected stolen laptop.

Doing Business over the Internet

Certificate Authorities

Business is built on trust. On the Internet that trust is easily compromised. To secure your data over the Internet, certificate authorities (CA) are the only way to go (Bruno, 1998). A CA with software that can generate and manage digital certificates can either be built in-house or outsourced to a third party. To build an in-house CA server, you must:

- Have a good working knowledge of public-key cryptography
- Decide on either top-down CA or cross-certification
- Weigh performance and scalability
- Make sure the CA software uses a standard certificate to ensure that different packages can communicate
- Make CAs comply with LDAP (lightweight directory access protocol) to make it easier to store certificates
- Decide on price and protection
- Decide on whether to control your own security

In deciding whether to outsource CA, you must:

- Decide on what people and budget it takes to support certificates
- Analyze the speed of deployment
- Leverage the third party's expertise and high-security facilities
- Determine if the burden of handling CA should be placed on a third party
- Decide on whether to control your own security
- Decide which third party is most trustworthy in its policies and practices

Whether developed in-house or outsourced, a CA has a straightforward task: It verifies the identities of end-users by issuing certificates—unique, encrypted, digital Ids—that are attached to e-mail, transaction records, or files sent over the Internet or Intranet (Bruno, 1998). A certificate is like a digital passport that lets the recipient know that the sender is who he or she claims to be.

All CAs are based on public-key cryptography; they typically have three components:

- *A database* that stores public keys
- *A cryptographic engine* that generates the actual certificate
- *A PKI (public key infrastructrure) engine* that tracks the expiration date of issued certificates

E-mail Security

E-mail has become such an integral part of the working world that it also poses significant security threats. The accessibility given by the Internet provides hackers with a direct line to personal and corporate in-boxes (Paone, 1999). Malicious code can be attached to incoming messages; a simple mouse click by the targeted user is all it takes to activate them. Spam (junk e-mail) can flood in-boxes with time wasting, unnecessary, or inappropriate content (Paone, 1999). Spam attacks can clog LANs or strain the Internet gateway.

Yet many companies and individuals do not give much thought to e-mail security. Unlike other security initiatives, e-mail is a more ongoing challenge than installing a firewall (Paone, 1999). One tool that can be used in desktop and corporate settings is virus-scanning software, but there is no single methodology that can protect against all e-mail-based threats (see Table 4.4).

TABLE 4.4: E-mail Security Holes

Vulnerability	Problem	Possible solutions
Unencrypted e-mail	Can be read by unknown and unauthorized third parties while it traverses the Internet, or even by unauthorized employees within the Internet	E-mail encryption, virtual private networking solutions
Malicious attachments and viruses	Unsuspecting users may open e-mail attachments from unfamiliar senders and unleash viruses or malicious active content onto their desktops	Virus scanning products for both the client and the firewall
Spam	More of a nuisance than a security problem, spam (junk e-mail) can clutter the LAN and in-boxes with unwanted and often inappropriate messages	E-mail filters

Source: Paone, 1999

Regardless of policies and products, e-mail security will remain a moving target as hackers continue to find their way around existing barriers. Some suggestions for securing e-mail include:

- Not opening attachments from unfamiliar sources
- Reporting instances of spam
- Using encryption when sending highly sensitive information across the Internet

Access Control

Access control is the mechanisms and policies that restrict access to computer resources. If an unauthorized user has physical access to your computer, that person can usually bypass a password-protected screen by rebooting the computer. Symantec Corporation has a product called Norton Your Eyes Only for Windows 95 that gives PC users easy, secure, and integrated access control. Your Eyes Only addresses the following security needs:

- Public/private key on-the-fly encryption/decryption
- Centralized management
- Mobile and remote users
- Access control for multiple users of a single machine

Your Eyes Only is available in two versions, one for end users and one for administrators. It uses public/private key technology to encrypt and decrypt files. A user who enters a password gains access only to his or her private key. Your Eyes Only lets you select key lengths of between 360 and 2,048 bits. It offers on-the-fly encryption and decryption that works automatically within applications as files are opened and closed.

Your Eyes Only offers the following access control features:

- *BootLock:* protects the boot process from unauthorized users, allowing Windows 95 users to lock an entire PC so that unauthorized users cannot start it even from a floppy disk.
- *ScreenLock:* protects the system while the user is temporarily away. It blanks the screen and locks access to the PC.
- *SmartLock folders:* offer on-the-fly encryption. You can specify the encryption method and the files to lock. Any files in SmartLock folders are automatically decrypted when opened and encrypted when closed.

Remote Access via the Internet

Most companies still use costly private dial-up to connect remote users. In addition, companies must install and configure encryption and tunneling software for a large number of mobile users. Sun Microsystems i-Planet is designed to leverage the cost of computing and offer access to your corporate Intranet from the Internet.

i-Planet software uses Java to eliminate the need for remote users to dial into a corporate modem pool or use security and authentication software tied to a laptop. By using the Internet standard for remote access, i-Planet enables remote users to access the private network from various technologies, such as cable modems, DSL, or ISDN (see Figure 4.19). With i-Planet users can use any browser enabled with Java technology to read e-mail, download data, check appointment calendars, and access other enterprise information.

FIGURE 4.19: i-Planet Topology

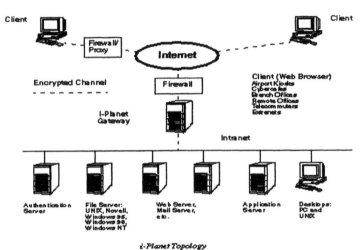

i-Planet Topology

Source: Sun Microsystems

The i-Planet architecture is a server software-based solution that does not require any client installation, management, or configuration; users need only a Web browser and an Internet connection. The client application is either pushed to the client as HTML Web pages or Java applet that is downloaded on demand. Once users clear the authentication, i-Planet creates a VPN on the fly. Authentication is handled over an encrypted SSL channel between the client Web browser and the i-Planet authentication system.

i-Planet software offers remote access security for:

- *Internal HTML front ends and Web sites*
- *E-mail access*
- *Calendar access*, supporting the Common Desktop Environment (CDE) calendar and Sun Calendar Server applications

- *X11 and PC applications*, allowing you to run existing mission-critical PC or X11 applications without any change

- *File access*, optimizing mail of large files and attachments by delegating as many tasks to be performed on the server as possible

- *Terminal emulation*, using local Telnet client and VT100 emulator to allow encrypted Telnet sessions from the Internet

Summary

Today computer security has to do with protecting your sensitive information from both outsiders and insiders. You need a security policy that covers all risks. Security tools such as firewalls, anti-virus software, and encryption will help your company deter access to unauthorized users.

Believing that your environment is secured is not enough. You have to take a proactive approach to security, making sure that newer technologies are implemented to keep up with sophisticated hacker tools. A safe and secure computer environment will protect your investments for the coming years.

References

An Analysis of Security Incidents on the Internet, 1989-1995, *www.cert.org*, April 17, 1997.

Backman, Dan, "Smartcards: The Intelligent Way to Security," *Network Computing*, *http://www.nwc.com/909/909w5/2.html*, May 15, 1998.

Bhimani, Anish, "All Eyes on PKI," *Information Security*, *www. infosecurity.com*, October 1998.

Bruno, Lee, "Certificate Authorities, Who Do You Trust?" *Data Communications*, Mar. 21, 1998, pp. 54-61.

Chapman, D. Brent, & Zwicky, Elizabeth D., *Building Internet Firewalls* O'Relly & Associates, Inc., 1995).

Foote, Steven, "19 Infosecurity Predictions for '99," *www.inforsecurity mag.com/nov/cover.htm*. 1998.

Garfinkel, Simson, & Spafford, Gene, *Practical UNIX & Internet Security*, O'Relly & Associates, Inc., June 27, 1999.

"A Gauntlet Firewall Executive White Paper," *www.nai.com/media/ doc/products/gauntlet_adaptiveproxy.doc*.

Innovative Security Products, *www.wesecure.com*, 1998.

An Introduction to Computer Security: The NIST Handbook, Special Publication 800-12, *http: //csrc.ncsl.nist.gov/nistpubs/800-12/*, February 7, 1996.

M2 Presswire, "Hewlett-Packard: HP corporate PCs, notebooks, workstations now optimized for smart cards," Nov. 18, 1998.

McCooey, Eileen, "Security Becomes Priority," *Windows Magazine* (Jan. 1, 1999), p. 50.

National Institute of Standards and Technology, *Computer Security Handbook Cryptography*, *http://security.isu.edu/isl/hk_crypt.html*.

Network Associates Executive White Paper, "The Active Firewall," *http://www.nai.com/international/uk/asp_set/products/tns/active security/acts_literature.asp*, August 18, 1999.

Paone, Joe, "Slaying the E-mail Demons: Making Mail Safe," *MicroTimes* (Apr. 2, 1999), pp. 117-27.

Pasmore, Frank, "Weaving a Secure Web," *Information Security*, *www.infosecuritymag.com*, 1999.

Perez, Juan Carlos, "IDC: Internet security market grows by $1 billion," *InfoWorld Electric, http://www.infoworld.com/cgi-bin/displaystory. pl?990330.ensecurity.htm,* Mar. 30, 1999.

Smart Cards, *www.microsoft.com*, Mar. 24, 1999.

Yasin, Rutrell, "Better Snapshots of Enterprise Security," *InternetWeek* (Feb. 22, 1999), p. 23.

Websites for Computer Security

Aladdin Knowledge Systems: *http://www.aks.com/*

AXENT Technologies, Inc.: *http://www.axent.com/*

Biometric Consortium: *http://www.biometrics.org/*

Chrysalis-ITS Security Assurance White Paper: *http://www. chrysalis.com/read/VPNwhitepaper.htm*

Cisco Systems, Inc.: *http://www.cisco.com/*

Computer Security Products, Inc.: http: *www.computersecurity.com/*

Computer Viruses—an Executive Brief, *http://www.symantec. com/avcenter/reference/corpst.html*

Deltavision: *http://www.deltavision.com/*

Entrust Technologies, Inc.: *http://www.entrust.com/*

Kerberos: The Network Authentication Protocol: *http://web.mit.edu/kerberos/www/*

Network Associates, Inc.: *http://www.nai.com/*

NIST Computer Security Resource Clearinghouse: *http://csrc.nist.gov/*

Security Information: *http://www.zdnet.com/devhead/filters/security/*

Sensar, Inc.: *http://www.sensar.com/*

Shumann Security Software, Inc.: *http://www.schumannsoftware.com/*

Sun Microsystems i-Planet: *http://www.swest2.sun.com/software/cover/*

Symantec Security Center: *http://www.symantec.com/avcenter/security/index.html*

Chapter 5
Personnel Security

Every staff position that interacts with the computer system should be evaluated from a security perspective. Establish criteria for filling each position; spell out the process to be used to evaluate candidates, screen applicants, and conduct background checks. Specify the training program for new employees.

Define each position clearly, describing its functions. Assess the sensitivity level. Sensitivity level is determined by the degree of harm a person could cause in that position: For instance, a person might be in a position to steal or disclose confidential data, interrupt critical processing functions, commit fraud, or steal resources. What type of computer access will be needed for the position? Employees should be given only the access needed to perform their duties.

Segregation of duties is an important control to ensure that employees do not perform incompatible duties. This means you must allocate responsibilities so that a single employee cannot perpetrate an error and cover it up in the normal course of his or her duties. You'll need checks and balances to prevent or catch irregularities, so that the duties of one person automatically check the work of another.

Functions such as systems analysis, programming, computer operations, and data control should be segregated. The electronic data processing (EDP) department should be organizationally independent of the operating departments. It should not have the authority to correct data entered by users in other departments.

Screening

Before you hire anyone for a sensitive position, perform a pre-employment background check. (For less sensitive positions, post-employment screening may be sufficient.) For highly sensitive positions, the background check should provide positive evidence that the candidate can perform the duties required honestly.

The applicant's prospective supervisor should not conduct the background check; the personnel department or an independent agency should do it.

A significant percentage of applicants lie either on resumes or in interviews. These individuals should be rejected not only because they may not be qualified but also because they lack the integrity required for sensitive positions.

Many individuals will not divulge a criminal past to prospective employers. If the employees thereafter commits a criminal act that affects others, the employer may be held liable. Employers have a legal obligation to thoroughly investigate their employees' backgrounds—without violating an employee's privacy. Check an applicant's previous address, professional and bank references, credit history, criminal record, and previous employers.

When applicants lie about their work history, they tend to:

- Increase the amount of time they have spent at a job
- Create fictitious employers
- Boost their salary levels
- Tell you that their employer has gone out of business
- Exaggerate job duties and inflate job titles
- Falsely claim to be self-employed or independent consultants

Candidates may also fabricate educational credentials and professional experience. Having only a year or two of college, they may claim that they have a degree. A person may have even assumed the identity of a real graduate or an established professional. Candidates may have bought their degrees from unaccredited mail-order universities. Some fabricate honors and awards. Others may list fake publications on their resumes. Applicants should be asked to provide copies of their publications and proofs of honors and awards.

Many employers do a poor job of checking references. They either don't bother with the references or ask superficial questions. To avoid legal hassles, all applicants should be required to sign a release form. The applicants should promise to hold their references harmless for what they say. Before any formal offer is made, if the reference check is not acceptable, it's not necessary to give the candidate a specific reason for not being chosen. Keep records of reference checks to refute allegations of discriminatory or illegal actions. A conscientious reference check may also defend your company in any later litigation over that employee's actions.

You can access hundreds of public sources to check an applicant's background. Checking from public sources does not require the applicant's permission. Public records often contain conviction records and in some jurisdictions arrest records.

Federal agencies collect a vast amount of data on individuals. The FBI's Identification Division contains the largest repository of criminal records in the United States. The Freedom of Information Act (FIA) allows you to access many government files, including criminal conviction records. A conviction in itself is generally not a sufficient reason to deny the applicant the job; the conviction should relate to the job you're trying to fill.

The financial and credit records of prospective applicants can be accessed through credit bureaus and private investigative agencies. The Fair Credit Reporting Act governs investigative consumer reports, which are frequently used by prospective employers to screen candidates.

Corporate records and limited partnership records are public. These records are one way to tell if the applicant actually owned a business, and for how long.

From court records, you can learn if the applicant was a participant in any civil or criminal litigation. City and county filings may give you information about such financial factors as whether there are any liens against the applicant. Additional sources of financial information are real property records and tax rolls. Financial situation may have an effect on a person's ability to perform the job; a financially troubled candidate may have a greater incentive to commit fraud.

The following companies perform pre-employment background verification:

- Accurate Data Services: *http://www.acudata.com/*
- Alexander Information Group: *http://www.alexinfogp.com/*
- American Background: *http://www.americanbackground.com/*
- American Labor Resources: *http://www.amlabor.com/*

- Application Profiles, Inc.: *http://www.ap-profiles.com/*
- Background Check International, LLC: *http://www.bcint.com/*
- Barrientos & Associates: *http://www.emcsat.com*
- Confidential Research Associates: *http://www.mrjcomp.com/cra/*
- Employment Research Service: *http://www.employment-research. com/*
- EMPFacts Factual Data: *http://www.employmentscreen.com/*
- Indepth Profiles: *http://www.idprofiles.com/*
- Informus Corp.: *http://www.informus.com/*
- Integri-Net: *http://www.integri-net.com/*
- Justifacts: *http://www.justifacts.com/*
- On-Line Screening Services, Inc.: *http://www.onlinescreening. com/*
- Pennell & Associates: *http://www.pennellinvestigations.com/*
- PEV: *http://pev.frickco.com/*
- Pre-Employment Screening, Inc.: *http://www.ddpes.com/*
- RCE Information Services: *http://www.iglou.com/datadetective/*
- SafeHands: *http://www.safehands.com/*
- StafTrack: *http://www.staftrack.com/*
- USDatalink: *http://www.usdatalink.com/*

Legal Agreements

Insist that new hires in sensitive jobs sign employment agreements with non-disclosure provisions. The agreement should specify:

- Scope of the employee's duties
- That the employee will work solely for your organization and may not work anywhere else without advance written permission
- That the organization is entitled to reap the benefit of the employee's work product
- That the employee will not reveal secrets to unauthorized individuals, within as well as outside the organization

- The conditions for terminating the employee
- That the employee will return all materials, including notes, handbooks, computer programs, commercial documents, and software at your request, and always at the end of the employment term
- That the employee may not keep any copies of items owned by the organization
- The limitations on the types of work the employee may do after leaving the organization
- That the employee will not engage in any unfair business practices, including corporate spying or engaging in a business that competes with the employer's business
- That the employee will abstain from any activity that may hurt the employer or its interests

Training New Employees

Training new employees in computer security responsibilities and duties is a highly effective way of enhancing security. You may want to limit a new employee's access to the computer systems till security training is completed, but it's also essential that computer security training be ongoing.

These are some of the issues to be addressed during training:

- The organization's data back-up policies
- The type of data that should be encrypted
- How the data encryption keys are managed
- What types of data may be shared with colleagues
- What types of data are available to the public

Performance Appraisal

Performance and skill level of employees should be routinely documented, using formal performance evaluation systems. Give employees feedback about their performance regularly.

An effective review procedure can help prevent job frustration and stress. It can also help maintain employee morale. It's important to be concerned about the threat of psychological dissatisfaction. Disgruntled employees may do intentional damage. Moreover, job turnover associated with dissatisfied employees disrupts the operation and maintenance of computer systems. Discontent can act as a catalyst for computer crime or sabotage. Watch for possible indicators of discontent, such as:

- Low quality or low production output
- Complaints
- Late arrivals
- Excessive absenteeism
- Putting off vacations
- Excessive unwarranted overtime

Quick action, like communicating with the employee on a one-to-one basis, can significantly minimize job discontent.

Exit Procedures

Special security issues arise when an employee leaves. An employee may leave on mutually agreeable terms, including retirement, promotion, accepting a better position at another company, or transferring willingly to another department. An employee may also leave on unfriendly terms, as when the employee is fired, unwillingly transferred to another department, forced into retirement, or demoted.

For a mutually agreeable termination, follow a standard exit procedure. Upon leaving the organization, employees should be required to return badges, keys, and company materials. Change their access codes and passwords, and even locks if necessary.

Data files, especially encrypted files and the keys to decrypt them, other documents, and all backed-up files should be returned. Don't let the employee keep copies of anything; you should both sign an agreement attesting that all copies have been returned.

Employees an cause considerable damage if terminated, for example, they may:

- Intentionally input erroneous data
- Erase data files and destroy back-ups
- Make copies of data files for personal use or for competitors
- Misfile or destroy important documents

• Create "random" errors that are difficult to trace and costly to correct

While most employees can do *some* harm to the computer system, systems personnel can do the most. From a security perspective, termination of systems personnel requires great caution. For example, systems personnel may delete or destroy data or program files. They may also place logic bombs to harm the system (erase data, deny access, etc.), activating the code after their departure. They can set these in place long before they're even notified of termination. Protect your organization with controls over modification of system files.

When an employee is leaving on unfriendly terms, his or her access to the computer system should be restricted as quickly as possible. These accounts should be closed before or at the same time as the employee is notified of the termination.

Chapter 6
Network Security

Networks may be broadly classified as either wide area networks (WANs) or local area networks (LANs). Security is needed for both. Computers in a WAN may be thousands of miles apart; computers in a LAN are usually closer together, such as in the same building or plant. Data-switching equipment may be used in LANs but not as often in WANs.

On the Internet security is needed to prevent unauthorized changes to your Web site. Businesses selling information-related products over the Internet, such as software vendors that allow their paying customers to download upgrades, need a way to discriminate between paying customers and visitors not paying.

Security administrators face the risk that an attacker will be able to break into the network. The attacks may range from direct attacks by both hackers and insiders to automated attacks using network worms. Such an attacker might:

- *Read access:* Read or copy confidential information.

- *Write access:* Write to a network—perhaps infecting the system with a virus or plant Trojan horses or back doors. The attacker may also destroy confidential information by deleting it or writing over it.

- *Denial of service:* Deny authorized users normal network services. An attack may consume CPU time or network bandwidth or fill up memory.

Security risks in using a server on the Internet include inappropriate configuration of FTP (file transfer protocol) settings. If FTP access to your server is allowed, configure it to prevent unauthorized modifications to files.

There must be a secure communication link for data transmission between interconnected host computer systems of the network. A major form of network communication security is cryptography to safeguard transmitted data confidentiality. Cryptographic algorithms may be either *symmetric* (private key) or *asymmetric* (public key).

The two popular encryption methods are *link-level* and *end-to-end* security. The former safeguards traffic independently on every communication link; the latter safeguards messages from source to destination. Link-level enciphers the communications line at the bit level, deciphering it as it enters the nodes. End-to-end enciphers information at the entry point to the network, deciphering it at the exit point, thus providing security over information inside the nodes.

You should have a list of authorized users, general or specific:

- Who is allowed into the facilities?
- When may they enter?
- For what purposes may they enter?

A variety of tools is available to help the IT manager implement the security plan, including encryption tools, route and packet filtering, and firewalls.

You must have a network security policy. Your company also needs an internal corporate security policy, once you decide how critical it is to protect the integrity of the computing system and the security of your Web site.

The internal security plan should be distributed to everyone who uses the facilities, with written guidance for employees on the proper use of passwords. Tell them the types of words that should not be used as passwords, and the policy about how often the password is to be changed.

There must be positive authentication before a user can access a terminal, an on-line application, or the network environment, and you may want date and time constraints. Your employees should have access to information only on a need-to-know basis. Unauthorized use should deactivate or lock a terminal. Diskless workstations may give you a safer environment.

Passwords

Most LAN or communication software packages contain encryption and security features. Passwords are included in virtually every package. However, people generally don't select good passwords or change them often enough. Hackers can easily breach security by guessing passwords.

The effectiveness of passwords is greatly diminished when users do not select good passwords. People tend to make certain mistakes. They share them with other individuals or write them down. If you need to write down a password to remember it, the purpose is defeated. These are good guidelines for choosing passwords:

- Don't choose a password that's a word or a name in English or any other language. Hackers often use dictionaries to find out passwords.

- Avoid patterns like 123456, 12468, asdf, or qwerty (from the keyboard).

- Don't use geographical names like Vegas or Florida.

- If your system requires that the password contain both numerals and letters, don't just add a number to a word. Hackers know that most people will choose a word and add the numeral one (e.g., CAT1 or 1CAT).

- Encourage a combination of upper and lower-case characters. Non-alphabetic characters also make it more difficult for hackers to guess passwords.

- An excellent technique is to use the first letter of a phrase to create a password. For example, "I Was Born In New York" would yield the password IWBINY. Although not a word that's easy to guess, it's easy to remember.

- Change passwords regularly; encourage this by programming the computer system to require new passwords. The system should keep a history of older passwords and check to ensure that users don't use the same password again or choose one they've used recently.

Give users security guidelines and give new users a course in security precautions and how to select a good password. Users must understand why a good password is essential. The Web site of Symantec, makers of security software, advises about selecting a good password, so users can evaluate the strength of the ones they choose: *http://www. symantec.com/avcenter/security/passwords/passwordanalysis/html*

Passwords provide good protection from casual or amateur hackers, but experienced hackers can typically bypass the password system, especially in the UNIX environment. Software programs are available to assist new hackers, even those with limited knowledge, to find or guess passwords.

The aim of most hackers is to obtain unlimited access to the computer system, typically by:

- Finding bugs or errors in system software
- Taking advantage of an incorrect installation
- Looking for human errors

Many hackers are authorized users with limited access trying to get unlimited access. These hackers will have a valid user ID and password and will be looking for weaknesses in the system.

In most UNIX systems, passwords are stored in an encrypted file. Some systems use a shadow password file where the original data is stored. Passwords are generally encrypted using the data encryption standard (DES) algorithm.

The encryption method used is essentially irreversible. While it's easy to encrypt a password, it's extremely difficult, almost impossible, to decrypt it, but hackers can discover passwords through brute force, especially those that consist of only six lower-case characters. Passwords for accounts that are likely to attract hackers must obviously not consist only of lower-case characters.

A serious design flaw can sometimes result in the creation of a "universal" password, one that satisfies the requirements of the log-in program without the hacker actually knowing the correct password. In one case, for example, a hacker could enter an overly long password. It could overwrite the actual password, thus allowing the hacker access.

Modem Connections

Any time a user connects to the network using a modem, additional risks are introduced into the system. These can be minimized with dial-in modems.

Simply keeping the telephone number secret is not sufficient. The many hackers who dial in all the telephone numbers in an entire prefix could randomly discover yours.

In the past many companies used dial-back techniques to reduce modem risk. Nowadays, caller ID accomplishes the same objective. Essentially the network allows access only from pre-identified telephone numbers. The obvious disadvantage is that the telephone numbers of authorized users must be known in advance. This makes it difficult for users who travel.

Another way to minimize risk from dial-in modems is to use hardware encryption devices on both ends of the connection, but these tend to be expensive.

A good telecommunications software program will have numerous protocol options, enabling communications with different types of equipment. Some programs error check information or software programs received. Desirable features in telecommunications programs include menus providing help, telephone directory storage, and automatic log-on and redial.

Saboteur's Tools

While in recent years ingenious procedures have been developed to preserve computer security, many computer systems are still astonishingly insecure. Saboteurs have at hand a wide variety of techniques to overcome security, among them:

Trojan Horse: The saboteur places a hidden program within the normal programs of the business. The computer functions normally while the hidden program collects data, modifies programs and files, destroys data, or even causes a complete shutdown of operations. Trojan horses can be programmed to destroy all traces of their existence after execution.

Salami Techniques: The perpetrator adapts the computer program to cause very small changes that are unlikely to be discovered but whose cumulative effect can be substantial. For example, the perpetrator may steal 10 cents from the paycheck of each individual and transfer it to his own account.

Back Door or Trap Door: In developing a computer program programmers sometimes insert a code to allow them to bypass standard security procedures. Once the programming is complete the code, either accidentally or intentionally, may remain in the program. Attackers use this extra code to bypass security.

Time Bomb/Logic Bomb: A code may be inserted into a computer program that causes damage when a predefined condition occurs.

Masquerade: A computer program is written to simulate a real program, perhaps the log-in screen and related dialogue. When a user attempts to log in, the program captures the user's ID and password and displays an error message, prompting the user to log in again. The second time, the program allows the user to log in. The user may never know that the first log in was fake, to capture the access code.

Scavenging: Normally when the user "deletes" data, that information is not actually destroyed; instead, the space is made available for the computer to write on later. A scavenger may thus be able to steal sensitive data that the user thought had been deleted but that actually was still available.

Viruses: Viruses are like Trojan horses except that the illegal code can replicate itself. A virus can spread rapidly throughout the system; eradicating it can be expensive and cumbersome. To guard against viruses, take care in using programs from diskettes or in copying software from bulletin boards or outside the company. Use disks only from verified sources. The best precaution is to use a commercial virus scanner on all downloaded files before using them.

Data Manipulation: The most common and easiest way of committing fraud is to add or alter data before or during input. The best way to detect this is to use audit software to scrutinize transactions and review trails that indicate additions, changes, and deletions to data files. The use of batch totals, hash totals, and check digits can also help prevent this type of crime.

- *A batch total* is a reconciliation between the total daily transactions processed by the micro and manual totals determined by an individual other than the computer operator. Material deviations must be investigated.

- *A hash total* is found by adding values that would not typically be added together, such as employee and product numbers, so the total has no meaning other than for control purposes.

- *A check digit* is used to ascertain whether an identification number (e.g., account number, employee number) has been correctly entered by adding a calculation to the ID number and comparing the outcome to the check digit.

Piggybacking: Physical piggybacking to gain access to controlled areas occurs when an authorized employee goes through a door using a magnetic ID card and an unauthorized employee right behind also enters the premises. The unauthorized employee is then in a position to commit a crime. In electronic piggybacking, an authorized employee leaves a terminal or desktop and an unauthorized individual uses it to gain access.

Designing Secure Networks*

The architecture of a network includes hardware, software, information link controls, standards, topologies, and protocols. A protocol relates to how computers communicate and transfer information. There must be security controls for each component within the architecture to assure reliable and correct data exchanges. Otherwise the integrity of the system may be compromised.

In designing the network, it's necessary to consider three factors:

1. The user should get the best response time and throughput. Minimizing response time entails shortening delays between transmission and receipt of data; this is especially important for interactive sessions between user applications. Throughput means transmitting the maximum amount of data per unit of time.

2. The data should be transmitted within the network along the least-cost path, as long as other factors, such as reliability, are not compromised. The least-cost path is generally the shortest channel between devices with the fewest intermediate components. Low priority data can be transmitted over relatively inexpensive telephone lines; high priority data can be transmitted over expensive high-speed satellite channels.

3. Reliability should be maximized to assure proper receipt of all data. Network reliability includes the ability not only to deliver error-free data, but also to recover from errors or lost data. The network's diagnostic system should be able to locate component problems and perhaps even isolate the faulty component from the network.

Network Media

When you choosing a network medium, you need to consider:

---

*Shim et al, Information Systems Management Handbook, (N.J.: Prentice-Hall, 1999).

- Technical reliability
- The type of business you're in
- The number of people who will need to access data simultaneously
- Number of micros
- The physical layout of your current equipment
- Frequency of updating
- Compatibility
- Cost
- Geographic dispersion
- Network operating software and support
- Applications software
- Expandability (adding workstations)
- Restriction to PCs (or can cheaper terminals be used?)
- Ease of access in sharing equipment and data
- Need to access disparate equipment, like other networks and mainframes
- Processing needs
- Speed
- Data storage capability
- Maintenance
- Noise
- Connectivity mechanisms
- Ability of network to conduct tasks without corrupting data

Network Topologies

A network *configuration* or *topology* is the physical shape of the network, the layout of linked stations. A *node* is a workstation. A *bridge* is a connection between two similar networks. Network *protocols* are software implementations providing support for network data transmission. A *server* is a micro or a peripheral performing tasks such as data storage within a LAN.

Network servers are of several types. A *dedicated* server is a central computer used only to manage network traffic. A computer used simultaneously as a local workstation is called a *non-dedicated* server. In general, dedicated servers provide faster network performance because they do not take requests from local users as well as network stations. In addition, these machines are not susceptible to crashes caused by local users' errors. Dedicated servers are expensive; they cannot be disconnected from the network and used as stand-alone computers. Non-dedicated servers have a higher price-performance ratio for companies that need occasional use of the server as a local workstation.

The most common types of network topology are:

- The *hierarchical* topology (also called vertical or tree structure) is attractive for several reasons. The software to control the network is simple and the topology provides a concentration point for control and error resolution. However, it also presents potential bottleneck and reliability problems. Network capabilities may be completely lost if there is a failure at a higher level.

- The *horizontal* (or *bus*) topology popular in LANs offers simple traffic flow between devices. This topology permits all devices to receive every transmission; in other words, a single station broadcasts to multiple stations. The biggest disadvantage is that since all computers share a single channel, a failure in the channel results in loss of the network. One way to get around this problem is with redundant channels. Another disadvantage of this topology is that the absence of concentration points makes it more difficult to isolate faults. A bus network usually needs a minimum distance between taps to reduce noise. To identify a problem, each system element must be checked. A bus topology is suggested for shared databases but not for single-message switching. It employs minimum topology to fill a geographic area while at the same time having complete connectivity.

- The *star* topology is widely used for data communication systems. The software is not complex and controlling traffic is simple. All traffic emanates from the hub or the center of the star. Though similar to the hierarchical network, however, the star topology has more limited distributed processing capabilities. The hub routes data traffic to other components. It also isolates faults, which is relatively simple in this configuration. The potential of bottleneck at the hub may cause serious reliability problems, however. One way to enhance reliability is to establish a redundant backup of the hub node.

  A star network is best when there's a need to enter and process data at many locations with day-end distribution to different remote users. It's easy to identify errors in this system, since each communication must go through the central controller. Maintenance is easy if the central computer fails the network. There's a high initial cost because each node must be hooked up to the host computer in addition to the cost of the host. Expansion is easy: You only need to run a wire from the new terminal to the host computer.

- The *ring* topology sends data flows in a circular direction. Each station receives the data and then transmits it to the next. One main advantage is that bottlenecks like those in the hierarchical or star networks are relatively uncommon. The structure is organized. The primary disadvantage is that the entire network can be lost if the channel between two nodes fails. Establishing a backup channel can usually alleviate this problem. Other ways to overcome it are switches to automatically route the traffic round the failed node, or redundant cables.

    A ring network is more reliable and less expensive when there is minimal communication between terminals. This type of network is best when there are several users at different locations who have to access updated data on a continual basis, because multiple data transmissions can occur simultaneously. The ring network permits users to create and update shared databases. With a ring, however, there is greater likelihood of error compared to a star because numerous intervening parties handle data. In light of this, data in a ring system should make an entire circle before being removed from the network.

- The *mesh* topology is very reliable, though complex. Its structure makes it relatively immune to bottlenecks and other failures. The multiplicity of paths makes it relatively easy to route traffic around failed components or busy nodes.

LANs and WANs

WAN and LAN topologies usually take different shapes. A WAN structure tends to be more irregular. Since an organization generally leases lines at considerable cost, it attempts to keep them fully utilized. To accomplish this, data for a geographical area is often routed through one channel; hence the irregular shape of the WAN network.

The LAN topology tends to be more structured. Since channels in a LAN network are relatively inexpensive, the owners are generally not concerned with maximum utilization of channels. Furthermore, since LANs usually reside in a single building, the situation is inherently more structured. LANs are flexible, fast, and compatible. They maximize equipment utilization, reduce processing cost, reduce errors, and ease information flow.

LANs use ordinary telephone lines, coaxial cables, fiber optics, or other devices like interfaces. Fiber optics produce good performance and reliability but are of high cost. LAN performance depends on physical design, protocols supported, and transmission band-width. *Band-width* is the frequency range of a channel; it reflects transmission speed along the network. As more devices become part of a LAN, transmission speed decreases.

Two or more LANs may be connected. Each node becomes a cluster of stations (subnetworks). The LANs communicate with each other. Advantages of interfacing networks are that:

- Total network costs are lower.
- Individual subnetworks meet particular needs, increasing flexibility.
- More reliable and higher-cost subnetworks can be used for critical activities.
- If one LAN fails, the other still functions.

Disadvantages are that:

- Complexity is greater.
- Some network functions may not be able to cross network boundaries.

Communications Security

The communication systems used to link data between two or more sites should be reliable, private, and secure. Communication systems are easily affected by environmental factors, hardware malfunctions, and software problems. Attacks on computers that do not require physical access fall under the domain of communications security.

The increased use of computer technology has also increased dependence on telecommunications. All types of data—sound, video, and traditional—are transferred over networks. Communications security means ensuring that the physical links between the computer networks function at all times. This also means that during data transmission, breakdowns, delays, and disturbances must be prevented. Take care to prevent unauthorized individuals from tapping, modifying, or otherwise intercepting data transmission.

Six considerations in communications security are:

1. *Line security:* restricting unauthorized access to the communication lines connecting the various parts of computer systems.

2. *Transmission security:* preventing unauthorized interception of communications.

3. *Digital signatures:* authenticating the sender or message integrity to the receiver. A secure digital signature process is comprised of (1) a method of signing a document that makes forgery infeasible, and (2) validating that the signature is the one whose it purports to be.

4. *Cryptographic security:* rendering the information unintelligible if transmission is intercepted by unauthorized individuals. Security coding (encryption) of sensitive data is necessary. When the information is to be used, it can be decoded. A common coding method is DES. For even greater security, double encryption may be used: Encryption is processed twice using two different keys. (You may also encrypt files on a hard disk to prevent an intruder from reading the data.)

5. *Emission security:* preventing electromagnetic radiation from electronic devices. These emissions can be intercepted, without wires, by unauthorized individuals.

6. *Technical security:* preventing the use of devices such as microphones, transmitters, or wiretaps to intercept data transmissions. Security modems allow only authorized users to access confidential data. A modem may have graduated levels of security. Different users may be assigned different security codes. There can be password and call-back features. There may be built-in audit trails, allowing you to monitor who is accessing private files.

VANs offer both communication services and specialized data processing. Generally, a company has no direct control over a VAN's security. However, VAN security has a direct effect on the client's overall security.

Communication security may be in the form of:

- *Access control*, which guards against improper use of the network. For example, Kerberos commercial authentication software can be added to a security system to verify a user's existence by encrypting passwords transmitted around networks. Password control and other user authentication devices, like the SecurID from Security Dynamics (800-SECURID) or Vasco Data Security's Access Key II (800-238-2726).

Do not accept a prepaid call if it's not from a network user. Hackers don't typically spend their own funds. Review data communications billings and verify each host-to-host connection. Review all dial-up terminal users. Are the telephone numbers unlisted and changed periodically? Control specialists should try to make unauthorized access to the network to test whether the security is working properly.

- *Identification*, which identifies the origin of a communication within the network, as by digital signals or notarization.

- *Data confidentiality*, which prevents unauthorized disclosure of information within the communication process.

- *Data integrity*, which guards against unauthorized changes (e.g., adding, deleting) of data at both the receiving and sending points, as through cryptographic methods. Anti-virus software should be installed at both the network server and workstations to alert users when viruses are trying to enter the system.

- *Authentication*, which substantiates the identify of an originating or user entity within the network, verifying that the entity is actually the one being claimed and that the information being transmitted is appropriate. Examples of security controls are passwords, time stamping, synchronized checks, nonrepudiation, and multiple-way handshakes. Biometric authentication methods measure body characteristics. Keystroke dynamics is another possibility for identification.

- *Digital signature*, signing messages with a private key.

- *Routing control*, inhibiting data flow to network elements identified as unsecure, such as relays, links, or subnetworks.

- *Traffic padding*, analyzing data for reasonableness.

- *Interference minimization*, eliminating or curtailing radar/radio transmission interference. For a small network, one workstation may be used as the backup and restore for other nodes. In a large network, several servers may perform backups, since the failure of one could have disastrous effects on the entire system. Access to backup files must be strictly controlled.

Token-Ring and Ethernet Networks

Traditional token-ring and Ethernet networks work on the broadcast principle, sending information in units called frames. Each frame contains information about a variety of items, including the sender's and the receiver's addresses. The sender broadcasts a frame that every receiver can see.

At any given moment only one computer in the network is broadcasting and all others are receiving. Another computer may broadcast after the first is finished. While all machines on a network can see the broadcasting computer's frame, under ideal conditions only the computer whose address matches the receiver's address in the frame should be able to access the frame's contents.

Sniffers

Sniffers are programs designed to capture certain information. Network managers use sniffers to analyze network traffic and network statistics. Hackers, however, may use sniffers to steal information, such as passwords.

Certain actions can minimize sniffing risk. The most obvious is to limit access. If the hacker cannot access the LAN, sniffers cannot be used. However, because it's often possible to restrict access to networks too tightly, other alternatives should be considered.

Switched versions of token-ring and Ethernet networks may minimize sniffing. With a switched LAN, each user has his own port on the switch. A virtual connection is established with the destination port for each frame sent. If the destination address in the frame doesn't mach, the risk associated with sniffing is significantly reduced. Switched networks tend to be more expensive; completely switched networks are rare.

Probably the best way to minimize sniffing risk is data encryption. It's important that the key is never sent over the network. Traditional information, such as the time, is used to enhance the encryption scheme.

Data Flow

Data-switching equipment routes data through the network to its destinations. For instance, such equipment can route data around failed or busy devices or channels.

Routers at each site are used to communicate with routers at other sites. Routers provide information about the individuals and the resources available in the LAN. They're responsible for directing the flow of information. It's possible to configure the routers so that certain types, such as FTP or Telnet do not allow either incoming or outgoing access. It's also possible to enable or disable certain routers to receive information only from certain network addresses.

Route and packet filtering requires significant technical knowledge as well as time. Most routers don't provide a security or audit trail, even though you need to know:

- Who tried to break into the computer system
- How often they tried
- What means they used to attempt the break-in

Data Transmission

Data transmission between computers in a network uses one of three methods:

- *Simplex transmission* is in one direction only. An example is radio or television transmission. Simplex transmission is rare in computer networks.

- *Half-duplex transmission*, found in many systems, can flow in both directions but not in both at the same time. In other words, once a query is transmitted from one device, it must wait for a response to come back.

- *Full-duplex transmission* can transmit information in both directions simultaneously it doesn't have the stop-and-wait aspects of a half-duplex system. Because of its high throughput and fast response time, full-duplex transmission is common.

Security Layers

Security should be provided in different layers. Both networking facilities and telecommunication elements must be secure. Make sure you have controls over both host computers and subnetworks.

Network traffic may be over many subnetworks, each having its own security levels, depending on confidentiality and importance. Each may need different security services and controls. Note that security aspects of each subnetwork have to be distributed to the gateways so as to incorporate security factors into routing decisions.

Network Backup

Backup capability is especially important in networks so that if one computer fails another can take over the load. This might be critical in certain industries such as the financial.

Secure Sockets Layer

When Secure Sockets Layer (SSL) is enabled (see *http://developer1. netscape.com/docs/manuals/security/sslin/contents.htm*), a Web browser will display a lock or similar symbol to indicate that the data transfer is secure. Another way to tell if a Web site is secure is to look at its address: It should start with "https://" rather than simply "http://."

Most Web-based monetary transactions are secured using SSL. Many Web severe/client products support SSL connections. To transact business on the web, you need access to such a server as well as a digital certificate.

While using SSL for encryption greatly enhances security and confidentiality, it does slow the communication interchange: All the data has to be encrypted and then decrypted.

The SSL protocol was developed by Netscape. It operates by layering a security protocol on top of an underlying connection transport protocol such as HTTP, Telnet, NNTP, FTP, and TCP/IP. SSL is built into Netscape's client and server products.

When building a Web site, you can enable SSL by configuring a security-enabled http (https) process on the server. Web pages that require SSL access can be specified. Common Gateway Interface (CGI) routines can be written on the server side to integrate SSL into existing applications.

SSL provides data encryption, checks for data integrity, and provides server—and, if required, client—authentication for a TCP/IP connection. SSL is open and nonproprietary. Encryption, decryption, and authentication are transparent for applications using SSL.

SSL is used extensively to encrypt and authenticate communications between clients and servers on the Web. The transport layer security standard (TLS) of the Internet Engineering Task Force (IETF) is based on SSL.

You can confirm and authenticate an SSL server's identity when you send sensitive information, such as a credit card number, to the server. The digital certificate used to prove authenticity serves as the key to SSL. Anyone with the correct software can become a certificate authority (CA), but usually there are only certain trusted CAs that a Web browser is programmed to accept; VeriSign, Inc., is one of the best-known.

Public-key cryptography techniques may be used to check if a server's certificate and public ID are valid. Similarly, a server can check that the client's certificate and public ID are valid. Without public-key cryptography, encrypted communication could take place between two or more users only if they shared the keys. Each user would have to maintain several keys for communicating with various users.

Public-key cryptography (see Chapter 4) allows parties to communicate securely without sharing secret keys. Each party establishes a key pair: one private key and one public key. The public key is available to all nodes on a network; it's used to encrypt messages to the node. The private key used to decrypt the messages never leaves its node.

TCP/IP (the Transmission Control Protocol/Internet Protocol) provides the rules for transporting and routing data over the Internet. Protocols like the HyperText Transport Protocol (HTTP) use TCP/IP to carry out tasks like displaying Web pages. The SSL protocol runs in the middle between TCP/IP and higher-level protocols like HTTP, allowing SSL-enabled clients and servers to authenticate themselves and making an encrypted connection possible.

The "strength" of an SSL connection depends on the bit level: 40-bit SSL connections tend to be weak; a 128-bit SSL connection is extremely strong. 128 bits is approximately 340 septillion times (340,000,000,000,000,000,000,000,000) larger than 40 bits.

It's presently illegal for US companies to export internationally anything above a 56-bit encryption. Software security companies are trying to overcome these restrictions by developing encryption technology outside the United States.

The SSL protocol includes two subprotocols. The SSL Record Protocol defines the format that will be used for data transmission. The SSL Handshake Protocol determines how the record protocol will exchange data between server and client when the SSL connection is first established. It's used to either authenticate the server to the client or the client to the server. It also allows client and server to select from cryptographic algorithms or ciphers supported by both client and server.

Public-key and symmetric key encryption are both used by the SSL protocol. While symmetric key encryption tends to be faster, public-key encryption provides better authentication. Common ciphers are:

- *Data Encryption Standard (DES)*. Triple DES applies DES three times and supports 168-bit encryption. Its key size makes it one of the strongest ciphers supported by SSL.

- *Digital Signature Algorithm (DSA)*, for authentication of digital signatures.

- *Key Exchange Algorithm (KEA)*, for key exchange.

- *Message Digest (MD5)*, used to create digital signatures. It is a commonly used cipher.

- *RSA*, a company name for authentication and encryption. RSA key exchange algorithm is common for SSL connections; it's the most popular cipher for commercial applications.

- *Secure Hash Algorithm (SHA-1)*, for secure data transmission.

- *SKIPJACK*, a classified symmetric-key algorithm used in FORTEZZA-compliant hardware. The FORTEZZA encryption system is used by US government agencies for sensitive but not classified data. FORTEZZA ciphers use KEA instead of RSA. FORTEZZA cards and DSA are used for client authentication.

Performance can suffer when using public-key cryptography, so it's usually limited to digital signatures or small amounts of data. Symmetric key encryption, such as DES, is typically used for bulk data.

Your security administrator should decide which cipher suites to enable or disable considering the nature of the data, the need for confidentiality and security, and the speed of the cipher. The national origin of the parties is another consideration; certain ciphers may only be used within the US and Canada. Thus, if your organization disables the weaker ciphers, you automatically restrict access to clients within the US and Canada.

SSL Handshake

The following sequence of events is typical in an SSL connection:

- The client provides the server with its own SSL version number, cipher settings, and other communications-related data.

- The server provides the client with its SSL version number, cipher settings, and other communications-related data.
- The server sends its certificate, requesting the client's certificate, if necessary.
- The client authenticates the server. If the server cannot be authenticated, the client is warned that an encrypted and authenticated connection cannot be established.
- The client creates a "pre-master" secret for the SSL connection and encrypts it with the server's public key. The encrypted pre-master is then sent to the server. The client may also be asked to sign and send data as well as its certificate to authenticate itself.
- The session will be terminated if the server cannot authenticate the client.
- The server uses its private key to decrypt the pre-master and generate the "master" secret using the pre-master.
- Using the master secret, session keys are generated by both client and server. These symmetric session keys are used to encrypt and decrypt the data. The keys ensure that the data is not tampered with between the time it's sent and the time it's received.
- The SSL session begins once the handshake is completed. Both client and server use the session keys to encrypt and decrypt data and to verify data integrity.

Authentication

Authentication of both clients and servers requires encrypting data with one key of a public-private key pair and decrypting it with the other. For server authentication the client encrypts the pre-master secret with the server's public key. The associated private key alone can decrypt the pre-master secret. This gives the client reasonable assurance about the server's identity.

To authenticate itself the client encrypts random pieces of data using its own private key. In other words, it creates a digital signature that can be validated, using the public key in the client's certificate, only if the corresponding private key had been used. If the server cannot validate the digital signature, the session will be terminated.

SSLRef

SSLRef is an advanced software developer's tool-kit to help provide security features in TCP/IP applications using the SSL protocol. ANSI C source code is provided for incorporation into TCP/IP applications. SSLRef may be downloaded free for noncommercial use. While there are no license restrictions on SSLRef, there are export restrictions.

Kerberos

The Kerberos protocol is used in a client/server environment to authenticate the client to the server and the server to the client. After authenticating identity, Kerberos may then be used to encrypt data. Kerberos does not send across any data that may allow an attacker to impersonate the user.

Kerberos is available free in the form of source code from the Massachusetts Institute of Technology and is also sold by several vendors in commercial software products.

When a client accesses a network service, the client asserts to the server that it's running on behalf of an authorized user. Without authentication, there's virtually no security. With Kerberos authentication, the client proves its identity to the server.

In the traditional environment, a user's identity is authenticated by checking the password during the log-in process. Without Kerberos authentication the user would need to enter a password to access each network service. This is at minimum inconvenient, and it still doesn't provide security when accessing services on a remote machine. Without encryption it would be easy for anyone to intercept the password during transit.

Kerberos eliminates the need to use passwords. Instead, a key is used to encrypt and decrypt short messages and provide the basis for authentication. The client, to prove its identity, presents a ticket issued by the Kerberos authentication server. Secret information, such as a password that only an authorized user would know, is contained in the ticket.

Kerberos is not effective against password-guessing attacks. A hacker who intercepts a few encrypted messages may launch an attack by randomly trying passwords to see if the messages decrypt.

Kerberos assumes that workstations or machines are reasonably secure and only the network connections are vulnerable. A trusted path for passwords is needed. For example, if the password is entered into a program containing a Trojan horse (that is, the program has been modified to capture certain information), Kerberos will not provide any protection. Moreover, if transmissions between the user and the authentication program can be intercepted, Kerberos will be ineffective.

Both the user and the network service must have keys registered with the Kerberos authentication server. The user's key is derived from the user-selected password. The network service key is selected randomly.

Many types of software used by the international community require Kerberos. Because the US restricts export of cryptography, a version of Kerberos called Bones is available for international users. All the DES routines have been stripped from Bones, which is used to "trick" other software into thinking that Kerberos is installed.

To use Kerberos, a Kerberos principal must be established. This principal is like a regular account on a machine; certain information, such as the user name and password, are associated with it. The information is stored encrypted in the Kerberos database. To be effective, Kerberos has to be integrated into the computer system. It protects only data from software that is configured to use it.

The server, if possible, should be physically secure. Ideally, the machine should be dedicated to running the authentication server. Access to the machine should be tightly restricted.

Each user's initial password has to be registered with the authentication server. The registration procedure depends on the number of users. In-person registration provides the best control if the number of users is small. Consider other procedures, such as a log-in program on a trusted system, when the number of users is large.

Several tools can enhance the security provided by Kerberos. One-time passwords generated by a device are particularly useful. Commercial products are available that combine one-time-passwords with Kerberos.

Sources of Information about Kerberos

Additional information about Kerberos is available from the following sites:

- *http://nii.isi.edu/info/kerberos/*
- *http://nii.isi.edu/publications/kerberos-neuman-tso.html*
- *http://www.cybersafe.com*
- *http://www.latticesoft.com>*
- *http://www.stonecast.net*
- *http://www.wrq.com*

Securing the DMZ

The *DMZ (demilitarized zone)* of a firewall deserves special attention (firewalls are explained in detail in Chapter 4). The DMZ is that part of the network that doesn't belong to either the internal network or the Internet. This is generally the area between the access router and the *bastion* host, a particularly vulnerable system that has been fortified against attacks (bastions may be part of the firewall).

Putting access control lists on the access router creates a DMZ. An access control list contains the rules that define which packets are permitted to enter. The access router, which connects an internal network with the Internet, is the first line of defense against attacks from the Internet.

If your system has different security levels, one option is to divide the DMZ into several separate zones so that, for instance, even an attacker who gains access will be unable to attack the private network because the bastion hosts are on a separate LAN.

Most organizations don't secure their Web servers strictly, so that unauthenticated users might be able to run CGI or other executable programs on the servers. If this is done on a bastion host, however, the entire security mechanism might be compromised.

Services should be split up not only by host but also by network, limiting the level of trust between hosts on the networks.

Use redundant components to achieve maximum security. A single failure, such as a software bug, should not compromise the entire system. Risk related to software bugs, for instance, can easily be reduced by:

- Keeping up to date on software fix patches
- Using well-known products that have been around a while
- Running only necessary services

If your emphasis is on maintaining security rather than allowing access, you may decide to block everything and allow access on a limited or case-by-case basis. In deciding which services to permit, ask yourself:

- What effect will allowing this service have on security?
- How does permitting the service affect firewall architecture?
- Will an attacker be able to exploit an inherent weakness?

- How well known is the service?
- Is the protocol for this service published?

Sources of Firewall Information

You can find more information about firewalls at:

- *http://sunsite.unc.edu/LDP/HOWTO/Firewall-HOWTO.html*
- *ftp://tp.tis.com/pub/firewalls/*
- *http://www.clark.net/pub/mjr/pubs/index.shtml*
- *ftp://ftp.research.att.com/dist/internet_security/*
- *http://www.net.tamu.edu/tfp/security/TAMU/*
- *http://www.cs.purdue.edu/coast/firewalls/*

Pretty Good Privacy (PGP)

Pretty Good Privacy (PGP) can be used to encrypt e-mail messages or digitally sign messages. If the encrypted e-mail is intercepted, it will appear to be garbage. Digital signatures can also be used when the content of the message isn't secret but the sender wants to confirm that he wrote it. PGP has proven very effective.

PGP relies on a public-key encryption scheme, but there's no need for a secure channel over which to secure the key. The public key used to encrypt the data is typically available in a public database. The decryption key is private.

PGP is available free for non-commercial use. ViaCrypt PGP, available for commercial use primarily in the US and Canada, costs under $100. For the international community, commercial PGP versions are available from Ascom Systec AG (IDEA@ascom.ch).

To use PGP, you need two key rings, one public and one private. The public ring holds your public key and the public keys of people known to you. The private ring holds your secret key or keys.

Public-key encryption is much slower than convention. PGP combines two algorithms, RSA and IDEA, to encrypt plain text. PGP's IDEA encryption scheme currently requires a 128-bit key. Using the fastest current technology, it would still take several trillion years to break the encryption scheme.

To launch a successful attack against such a scheme, an attacker would have to understand the mathematical transformation that takes place between plain and cipher text. The complexity of the transformation makes it extremely difficult to solve the mathematical problem.

At present PGP gives you three choices for key size: 512, 768, or 1,024 bits. It's also possible to specify the number of bits for your key. Increased key size means increased security, but key size also affects the program's running time during generation.

Only the RSA portion is affected by key size during encryption; the main body of the message is not affected. Therefore it's best to use the 1,024-bit key size. Note, though, that individuals running certain PGP versions may be unable to handle very large keys.

Each time PGP is run, a different session key is generated. This enhances security.

Using PGP, it's possible to apply a digital signature to a message. If a trusted copy of the sender's public key is available, it can be used to check the signature. It's impossible of anyone else to create the signature without the secret key. This will also detect if someone has tampered with the message.

If the contents of a message are not secret but it's essential to allow others to verify the identity of the sender, you may use *clear signing* digital signatures. Clear signing works only on text files, not on binary files.

You may sign someone's key if you wish to inform others that you believe the key belongs to that person. Other people may rely on your signature to decide whether or not that person's key is valid. A key-signing party is used to get together various users of PGP and extend the degree of trust on the Web.

If the secret key ring is stolen or lost, the key should be revoked. Using a backup copy of the secret key ring, a key revocation certificate may be uploaded to one of the public key servers. Before uploading the revocation certificate, it's a good idea to add a new ID to the old key to inform others what your new key ID will be. Without a backup copy of the secret key ring, it's impossible to create a revocation certificate.

Although there are several public key servers, it's only necessary to send your key to one of them. That server will send your key to the others. Keys may be submitted or extracted at: *http://pgp5.ai.mit.edu/*.

Sources of PGP Information

You can get further information about PGP at:

- *http://dir.yahoo.com/Computers_and_Internet/Security_and_ Encryption/PGP__Pretty_Good_Privacy/*
- *http://www.pgpi.com/links/*

- *http://home.epix.net/~alf/Security/*
- *http://web.mit.edu/network/pgp.html*
- *http://thegate.gamers.org/~tony/pgp.html*
- *http://www.nai.com/default_pgp.asp*

Security Analysis Tool for Auditing Networks

The Security Analysis Tool for Auditing Networks (SATAN) was written by Dan Farmer and Wietse Venema because computer systems are becoming more vulnerable to attacks via networks.

SATAN gathers information about a remote host or set of hosts by probing various services such as *Finger* or *FTP* provided by the host. It identifies potential security flaws and bugs, such as incorrectly configured network services or known system bugs.

SATAN consists of several programs, each testing for a specific weakness. Additional programs may be added by putting their executable file into SATAN's main directory. The entire SATAN package, including source code and documentation, is freely available via FTP from various sites, including:

SATAN Demo
- *http://www.fish/com/satan/*

North America
- *ftp://ftp.mcs.anl/gov/pub/security*
- *ftp://coast.cs.purdue.edu/pub/tools/unix/satan*
- *ftp://vixen.cso.uiuc.edu/security/satan-1.1.1.tar.Z*
- *ftp://ftp.acsu.buffalo.edu/pub/security/satan-1.1.1.tar.Z*
- *ftp://ftp.acsu.buffalo.edu/pub/security/satan-1.1.1.tar.gz*
- *ftp://ftp.net.ohio-state.edu/pub/security/satan/satan-1.1.1.tar.Z*
- *ftp://ftp.cerf.net/pub/software/unix/security/*
- *ftp://ftp.tisl.ukans.edu/pub/security/satan-1.1.1.tar.Z*
- *ftp://ftp.tcst.com/pub/security/satan-1.1.1.tar.Z*
- *ftp://ftp.orst.edu/pub/packages/satan/satan-1.1.1.tar.Z*
- *ftp://ciac.llnl.gov/pub/ciac/sectools/unix/satan/satan.tar.Z*

Australia

- *ftp://ftp.dstc.edu.au:/pub/security/satan/ satan-1.1.1.tar.Z*
- *ftp://coombs.anu.edu.au/pub/security/satan/*
- *ftp://ftp.auscert.org.au/pub/mirrors/ftp.win.tue.nl/satan-1.1.1. tar.Z*

Europe

- *ftp://ftp.denet.dk/pub/security/tools/satan/ satan-1.1.1.tar.Z*
- *http://ftp.luth.se/pub/unix/security/ satan-1.1.1.tar.Z*
- *ftp://luth.se/pub/unix/security/ satan-1.1.1.tar.Z*
- *ftp://ftp.wi.leidenuniv.nl/pub/security*
- *ftp://ftp.cs.ruu.nl/pub/SECURITY/ satan-1.1.1.tar.Z*
- *ftp://ftp.cert.dfn.de/pub/tools/net/satan/ satan-1.1.1.tar.Z*
- *ftp://ftp.csi.forth.gr/pub/security/ satan-1.1.1.tar.Z*
- *ftp://informatik.uni-kiel.de/pub/sources/security/MIRROR.ftp. win.tue.nl*
- *ftp://ftp.kulnet.kuleuven.ac.be/pub/mirror/ftp.win.tue.nl/security/*
- *ftp://ftp.ox.ac.uk/pub/comp/security/software/satan/satan-1.1.1. tar.Z*
- *ftp://ftp.nvg.unit.no/pub/security/ satan-1.1.1.tar.Z*
- *ftp://cnit.nsk.su/pub/unix/security/satan*

Courtney

Courtney, available free, may be thought of as the anti-SATAN. It monitors attacks from SATAN. Thus, if SATAN is probing your system, Courtney notifies you and gives you a chance to trace the probe. Courtney can be downloaded from:

http://ciac.llnl.gov.ciac/ToolsUnixNetMon.html#Courtney

Automated Vulnerability Testing

Generally, it's not that controls are lacking or weak but that they aren't appropriately configured. Most computer software, for example, comes with default settings. If these are left unchanged, security may be compromised.

The existence of controls gives management and users the false impression that their data is secure. Many hackers exploit well-known security weaknesses. They rely on common errors made by system administrators, such as not protecting the system with the latest security patches.

While incompetence or lack of time or other resources certainly contributes to this problem, many administrators make mistakes because of the nature of computer systems. Most systems support a wide variety of services, and the security mechanism must be flexible enough to meet the needs of a variety of users. This flexibility can often lead to security weaknesses.

Many automated tools audit computer systems and report potential security weaknesses. They can examine thousands of files on a multi-user computer system and identify vulnerabilities resulting from improper use of controls or mismanagement. Automated tools may test for adequate virus protection or for the ability to plant Trojan horses or worms.

Automated tools for testing security vulnerability are different from automated tools that monitor activity or detect intrusion. Monitors and intrusion detection systems analyze activity as it occurs. Vulnerability testing tools search for potential weaknesses.

Stand-alone Systems

To identify vulnerabilities in a stand-alone system, automated testing tools analyze shared executable files. Vulnerability testing tools are used to analyze files whose modification or disclosure would allow the hacker to circumvent system controls and gain unauthorized access.

The testing tools can check, for instance, if the passwords are long enough. Short passwords can be guessed easily using brute force. These tools can also check to see if passwords are changed often enough.

To prevent the planting of a Trojan horse program, user start-up files should be protected against modification, because the start-up files are always executed. Write-access in a user's personal file space should similarly be limited.

The audit trail should always be maintained. Automated tools can check to see if modification privileges for system binaries are restricted to systems staff. System binary files should be reviewed for unexpected changes, and secure defaults should be specified.

In a networked environment, computer systems generally share data and other resources. Security controls for access paths in networks can be tested. A network host will have the potential vulnerabilities not only of a stand-alone system but also of the networked system.

Testing Techniques

Vulnerability tests may audit the system or launch a mock attack. Testing thus may be passive or active, broad or narrow.

Active tests are intrusive; they identify vulnerabilities by exploiting them. *Passive* tests examine the system to infer the existence of vulnerabilities. An active test may launch a dictionary attack or randomly try common or short passwords. If successful, it would log the results for review by security personnel. A passive test might check the protection of a password file. It may copy the file, encrypt it, and compare encrypted strings. Both types of tests provide useful information. However, active tests are riskier. Individual circumstances and professional judgment affect the choice of tests.

Vulnerability testing programs may be *narrow*, examining only a single vulnerability, or *broad*, examining the entire system. While single vulnerability tests tend to be simple, they may not reveal the joint effect of lack of testing. Weaknesses in multiple controls may compound the effect of vulnerabilities. System testing provides better information than a series of single tests, making it easier to determine the total risk.

Conclusion

Computer networks play a dominant role in transmitting information within and between firms. A network is simply a set of computers (or terminals) connected by transmission paths. These paths are usually telephone lines but may be other media, such as wireless or infrared transmission, radio waves, or satellites. The network serves one purpose: exchange of data.

Encryption must be used whenever sensitive or confidential information is transmitted. The Internet network is so open that anything can be read or snatched at many locations between the originating site and the destination site. Encryption should be used when putting any secret or sensitive information on the Internet server.

In a networked environment, the more connections, the more complex the system—and the greater the likelihood of security being compromised.

Appendix 6.A: Commerical Firewalls*

Product Vendor	E-mail	OS/ Hardware Platforms	Contact Information
Actane Controller	info@actane.com	SNMP PC	Le California Bat D2 2, Rue Jean Andreani 13084 Aix-En-Provence CEDEX 2 France
AFS 2000 Internet Device Internet Devices	sales@internetdevices.com	-	(408) 541-1400
Alta Vista Firewall Alta Vista	-	WNT PC	-
Ascend Secure Access Firewall	info@ascend.com	PC	One Ascend Plaza 1701 Harbor Bay Parkway Alameda, CA 94502 USA (510) 769-6001
aVirt Gateway aVirt Gateway Solutions	sales@aVirt.com	PC	51 West Center, Suite 604 Orem, UT 84043 USA (800) 41-AVIRT or (801) 802-7450
BIGfire Biodata and AB Systems	sales@biodata.com.sg	-	Burg Lichtenfels D-35104 Lichtenfels, Germany Tel: ++49-6454-912070
BorderWare BorderWare Technologies	info@borderware.com	POS, PC	6695 Millcreek Drive, Unit 1 Mississauga, Ontario L5N 5R8 Europe: +44 181 893 6066 North America: 1 905 814 7900
Brimstone SOS Corporation	sales@soscorp.com	any PC	40 Broad Street, Suite 2175 New York, NY 10004 USA (800) SOS-UNIX or (212) 809-5900
Bull S.A.:Firewall and Netwall	-	UNIX/WS	-
Centri Cisco	info@cisco.com	WNT PC	170 W. Tasman Dr. San Jose, CA 95134 USA (408) 526-4000

Product Vendor	E-mail	OS/ Hardware Platforms	Contact Information
Cisco IOS Firewall Cisco	info@cisco.com	Router	170 W. Tasman Dr. San Jose, CA 95134 USA (408) 526-4000
Cisco PIX Cisco	info@cisco.com	POS	170 W. Tasman Dr. San Jose, CA 95134 USA (408) 526-4000
Citadel Citadel Data Security	info@cdsec.com	UNIX PC	Unit 3, 46 Orange Street Cape Town, 8001 South Africa Tel: +27 21 23-6065
Conclave Internet Dynamics	sales@interdyn.com	NT PC	3717 E. Thousand Oaks Blvd. Westlake, CA 91362 USA (630) 953-7706
CONNECT:Firewall Sterling Commerce	connect@sterling.com	SUN WS	4600 Lakehurst Court Dublin, OH 43016-2000 USA (800) 700-5579 or (33) 1 4417-6400
ConSeal PC Signal 9 Solutions	firewall@signal9.com	W95 PC	(613) 599-9010
COOL-FIRE Symbolic	mt@symbolic.it	-	Viale Mentana 29 I-43100 Parma, Italy Tel: +39 521 776180
CryptoSystem PyroWall RADGUARD	info@radguard.com	-	24 Raoul Wallenberg Street Tel Aviv 69719 Israel Tel: 972 3 645 5444
CSM Proxy Plus CSM-USA	Var_sales@csm-usa.com	Many PC WS	360 So. Ft. Lane Suite # 1B Layton, UT 84041 USA (801) 547-0914
CyberGuard CyberGuard Corporation	info@cybg.com	UNIX WS PC	2000 W. Commercial Blvd. Ft. Lauderdale, FL 33309 USA (954) 958-3900
Cybershield Data General	-	UNIX WS	(508) 898-5000

Product Vendor	E-mail	OS/ Hardware Platforms	Contact Information
CYCON Labyrinth CYCON Technologies	labyrinth@cycon.com	UNIX PC	11240 Waples Mill Rd., Suite 403 Fairfax, VA 22030 USA (703) 383-0247
Digital Firewall Service Digital Equipment Corp.	email directory	UNIX WNT	United States Contact: Dick Calandrella (508) 496-8626
DEC SecurityGate for OpenVMS[*] Digital Equipment Corp.	email directory	VMS -	contacts or (508) 568-6868
Elron Firewall Elron Software	info@elronsoftware.com	POS	One Cambridge Center Cambridge, MA 02142 USA (617) 692-3000
enterWorks NetSeer Light enterWorks.com	Michael Lazar	-	19886 Ashburn Road Ashburn, VA 20147 USA (800) 505-5144 or (703) 724-3800
ExFilter V1.1.2	exfilter@exnet.com or exfiler@exnet.co.uk	SUN WS	-
FLUX EF Enhanced Firewall INS Inter Networking Systems	flux-info@ins.de	FluxOS	INS GmbH P.O. Box 101312 D-44543 Castrop-Rauxel, Germany Tel: +49 2305 101 0
Firewall-1 Check Point Software Technologies	sales@CheckPoint.com	UNIX NT many	400 Seaport Court, Suite 105 Redwood City, CA 94063 USA (800) 429-4391
Firewall/Plus™ Network-1	sales@network-1.com Alyssa Earnhart	WNT DOS PC	(972) 606-8200 for Texas (800) 638-9751 World Headquarters
Fort Knox Firewall Device Internet Devices	sales@internetdevices.com	- PC	(408) 541-1400 x314
Freegate FreeGate Corporation	info@freegate.com	-	1208 E. Arques Sunnyvale, CA 94086 USA (408) 617-1000

Product Vendor	E-mail	OS/ Hardware Platforms	Contact Information
Gauntlet Trusted Information Systems Network Associates	tis@tis.com (us) info@eu.tis.com (non-us)	-	-
GEMINI Trusted Security Firewall Gemini Computers	tft@geminisecure.com	-	(408) 373-8500
GFX Internet Firewall System GNAT Box Global Technology Associates	gfx-sales@gta.com gb-sales@gta.com	UNIX/POS PC	3504 Lake Lynda Drive Suite 160 Orlando, FL 32817 USA (800) 775-4GTA or (407) 380-0220
GlobeServer Data Quest Information Systems	info@dqisystems.com	LINUX PC	7509 Kingston Pike Suite 313 Knoxville, TN 37919 USA (423) 588-4757
HSC GateKeeper Herve Schauer Consultants	info@hsc.fr	-	142, rue de Rivoli 75039 Paris Cedex 01 Tel: +33 (1) 46.38.89.90
IBM Firewall for AIX IBM	peter_crotty@vnet.ibm.com	AIX WS	IBM Internet Firewall PO Box 12195 Mail Drop B44A/B501 RTP, NC 27709 US Tel: +1 919-254-5074
ICE.Block J. River, Inc.	info@jriver.com	UNIX PC	124 North First Street Minneapolis, MN 55401 USA (612) 339-2521
Instant Internet Deerfield Communications	info@deerfield.com	WNT, W95 PC	(517) 732-8856
Interceptor Technologic	info@tlogic.com	- PC	4170 Ashford Dunwoody Rd. Ste. 465 Atlanta, GA 30319 USA (404) 843-9111
InterLock MCI Worldcom Advanced Networks	info@ans.net	SUN WS	1875 Campus Commons Dr. Reston, VA 22091 USA (800) 456-8267 or (703) 758-7700
Inter-Ceptor Network Security International	-	-	John Shepard at (516) 674-0238

Product Vendor	E-mail	OS/ Hardware Platforms	Contact Information
IPAD 1200 Netmatrix Internet Co.	sales@ipad-canada.com	POS	Netmatrix Corporation #36001, 6449 Crowchild Tr. Calgary, Alberta Canada T3E 7C6 (403) 686-1169
IRX Firewall Livingston Enterprises	info@livingston.com sales@livingston.com	Router	4464 Willow Road Pleasanton, CA 94588 USA (510) 737-2100
Iware Internetware	Paul Singh	Novell	505 W. Olive Ave., Suite 420 Sunnyvale, CA 94086 USA (408) 244-6141
iWay-One BateTech Software	www.workgroup.co.za sales@batetech.com	WNT -	7550 W. Yale Ave., B130 Denver, CO 80227 USA (303) 763-8333
Juniper Obtuse Systems	info@obtuse.com	-	Alberta, Canada
KarlBridge/KarlBrouter KarlNet Inc.	sales@KarlNet.com	Bridge/ Router	Columbus, OH USA (614) 263-KARL
Lucent Managed Firewall Lucent Technologies	firewall@lucent.com	WNT UNIX POS	480 Red Hill Road Middletown, NJ 07748 USA (800) 288-9785
MIMEsweeper Intergralis	info@us.integralis.com	WNT PC	UK: +44 (0) 1734 306060 US: (206) 889-5841
M>Wall MATRAnet	delplanque@matranet.com	UNIX WNT WS PC	18 rue Grange Dame Rose BP 262 - 78147 Velizy Cedex France Tel: +33 (0) 1 34 58 44 58
NetCS NetCS Informationstechnik GmbH	Oliver Korfmacher	Router	Katharinenstrasse 18 D-10711 Berlin, Germany Tel: +49.30/89660-0
NetGate™ SmallWorks	info@smallworks.com	SUN WS	(512) 338-0619
NetGuard Control Center (was Guardian) LanOptics	sales@lanoptics.com	WNT W95 PC	2445 Midway Rd. Carrollton, TX 75006 USA Tel: (972) 738-6900

Product Vendor	E-mail	OS/ Hardware Platforms	Contact Information
NetRoad/FireWARE/FireWALL Ukiah Software	-	WNT NWR PC	-
NetSafe Siemens Nixdorf	info@swn.sni.be	UNIX WS	SNS RD21 Rue de Niverlie 11 B-5020 Namur Belgium Tel: +32 (0) 81/55.47.00
Netscreen-100 Netscreen Technologies	info@netscreen.com	POS	4699 Old Ironside Drive Ste. 300 Santa Clara, CA 95054 USA Tel: (408) 970-8889
Net SecurityMaster SOLsoft SA	info@solsoft.com	UNIX WNT WS PC	4 bis, rue de la Gare 92300 Levallois-Perret France Tel: +33 147155 500
Netra Server Sun MicroSystems	-	SUN WS	SunSoft, Inc. 2550 Garcia Ave. Mountain View, CA 94043 (800) SUN-SOFT outside US: 1-415-960-3200
Network Systems ATM Firewall BorderGuard Network Control Facility The Security Router StorageTek Network Systems Group	webmaster@network.com	-	Tel: (800) NET INFO
Nokia IP & VPN Series Nokia Telecommunications	info@iprg.nokia.com	Router	232 Java Drive Sunnyvale, CA 94089 USA Tel: (408) 990-2000
Norman Firewall Norman Data Defense Systems	norman@norman.com	UNIX WS PS	3040 Williams Dr. 6th Floor Fairfax, VA 22031 USA (703) 573-8802
Novix FireFox	-	Novell	(800) 230-6090
Orion Zebu Systems	info@zebu.com	-	Samantha Agee (206) 781-9566

Product Vendor	E-mail	Hardware Platforms	Contact Information
Phoenix Adaptive Firewall Progressive Systems	info@progressivesystems.com	-	2000 W. Henderson Rd. Ste. 400 Columbus, OH 43220 USA (614) 326-4600
PORTUS & PORTUS-ES Livermore Software Laboratories	portusinfo@lsli.com	ALL ALL	1830 S. Kirkwood, Suite 205 Houston, TX 77077 USA (281) 759-3274
PrivateNet NEC Technologies	info@privatenet.nec.com	BSD UNIX	(800) 668-4869 Department Code: YCB
Pyramid Firewall DataTec	antoniob@datatec.co.uk	UNIX POS	650 Wharfedale Rd. Winnersh Wokingham Berkshire RG41 5TP UK Tel: 0118 925 6213
Quiotix	jbs@Quiotix.com	-	-
Raptor Axent Technologies	info@axent.com	UNIX, WNT WS, PC	2400 Research Blvd. Rockville, MD 20850 (888) 44-AXENT
SecureLan SecureAccess SecureFrame Cylink	-	-	8229 Boone Blvd., Suite 650 Vienna, VA 22182 USA (800) 449-1162
SecurIT Firewall Milkyway Networks	Info@milkyway.com	UNIX WNT WS PC	150-2650 Queensview Drive Ottawa, ON, Canada K2B 8H6 (800) 206-0922
Sidewinder, SecureZone, and Secure Computing Firewall for NT Secure Computing	sales@securecomputing.com	PC	Contact Info Worldwide Tel: +1 (408) 487-1900
Site Patrol BBN Planet Corp.	Gregg Lebovitz	-	-
SmartWall V-ONE	sales@v-one.com	-	20250 Century Blvd. Germantown, MD 20874 USA (301) 515-5200
SonicWall Sonic Systems	info@sonicsys.com	Any POS	575 N. Pastoria Ave. Sunnyvale, CA 94086 USA (408) 736-1900

OS/

Product Vendor	E-mail	Hardware Platforms	Contact Information
SPF-100/SPF-200 Sun MicroSystems	sunscreen@incog.com	POS WS, PC	Mountain View, CA 94043 USA (415) 960-3200
Sygate SyberGen	-	W95, WNT PC	-
Turnstyle Firewall System (TFS) Turnstyle Internet Module (TIM) Atlanta Systems Group	US Sales and Marketing Canada	UNIX -	US: (516) 737-6435 CAN: (506) 453-3505
VCS Firewall The Knowledge Group	sales@ktgroup.co.uk	UNIX PC	Concorde Road Patchway, Bristol UK Tel: ++44 (0) 117 900 7500
VPCom Ashley Laurent	Jeffrey Goodwin	UNIX NT	707 West Avenue, Suite 201 Austin, TX 78701 USA (512) 322-0676
Watchguard Watchguard Technologies	sales@watchguard.com	All PC	Contacts: (888) 682-1855 or (206) 521-8340
WebSENSE NetPartners Internet Solutions	sales@netpart.com	-	9210 Sky Park Court San Diego, CA 92123 USA (800) 723-1166 or (619) 505-3020
WinGate Deerfield Communications	info@deerfield.com	WNT, W95 PC	(517) 732-8856
ZapNet! IPRoute/Secure	info@iproute.com	WNT PC	Suite 400-120, 10945 State Bridge Rd. Alpharetta, GA 30202 USA (770) 772-4567

UNIX, LINUX, WIN= Windows, W95= Windows95, WNT= WindowsNT
POS= Proprietary or embedded operating system
WS= RISC-based workstation
PC= Intel-based personal computer

Appendix 6.B: Firewall Resellers

Company	Products/ Services	E-mail	Contact Information
ANR	NetGuard Control Center and Security consulting	info@anr.co.il	20 Admonit St. Netanya 42204 Israel Tel: 972-9-885-0480
Astra Network	Security and network consulting, Firewall installation & admin.	infosec@man.net	2633 Portage Ave. Winnipeg, MB Canada R3J 0P7 (204) 987-7050
Atlantic Computing Technology	BorderWare	info@atlantic.com	84 Round Hill Road Wethersfield, CT 06109 (203) 257-7163
ARTICON Information Systems GmbH	BorderWare	-	-
Bell Atlantic Network Integration	Network and firewall design	sales.lead@bani.com	52 East Swedesford Road Frazer, PA 19355 USA (800) 742-2264
BRAK Systems	Firewall-1, WebSENSE and others	tony@brak.com	1 City Centre Drive, Suite 801 Mississauga, Ontario Canada L6S 4T2 (905) 272-3076
Cadre Computer Resources	Firewall-1, Secured ISP, Internet development	info@ccr.com	3000 Chemed Center 255 East Fifth Street Cincinnati, OH 45202 (513) 762-7350
C-CURE	Information Security Architects	luc.dooms@c-cure.be	K. Rogierstraat 27 B-2000 Antwerpen Belgium Tel: +32 (0)3 216.50.50
Centaur Commucication GmbH	Firewall-1 and others, Security cosulting	info@centaur.de	Urbanstrasse 68 74074 Heilbronn Germany Tel: +49 7131 799 0
Citadel Security Management Systems	Gauntlet, many others, and Internet consulting	infocit@citadel. com.au	726 High Street Armadale, VIC AU Tel: 03 9500 2990

Company	Products/ Services	E-mail	Contact Information
CleverMinds	Gauntlet, others, and security consulting	Jack Boyle	Bedford, MA USA Tel: (781) 275-2749
Cohesive Systems	Centri Firewall Information services	info@gi.net	755 Page Mill Road Suite A-101 Palo Alto, CA 94304 USA (800) 682-5550
Comark	Firewall-1, and others, Security consulting	webteam@comark. net	444 Scott Drive Bloomingdale, IL 60108 USA Tel: (630) 924-6700
Comnet Solutions	Shareware firewall: Midiator One	firewall@comnet. com.au	ComNet Solutions Pty Ltd Unit 4/12 Old Castle Hill Road Castle Hill, NSW 2154 Australia Tel: +61 2 899 5700
Computer Software Manufaktur (CSM)	CSM Proxy & Proxy Plus Internet Gateway with fw features	sales@csm-usa.com	P.O. Box 1105 Layton, UT 84041 USA (801) 547-0914
Com Tech Communications	Firewall-1 and others Online Security Services	rof@comtech.com.au	Australia Tel: 0412 163374
Connect GmbH	SmartWall BorderGuard NetStalker and Virus Wall	Armin Bolenius	Pichlmayrstr. 26a D-83024 Rosenheim Germany Tel: +49-8031-219820
Collage Communications	Many firewalls and network services	cyberguard@Coll Com.COM	12 Tulip Lane Palo Alto, CA 94303 USA
Comcad GmbH	Firewall-1 others, and security and network services	frank.recktenwald@ comcad.de	Industriestr. 23 51399 Burscheid Germany Tel: +49-2174-6770
Conjungi	Gauntlet	simon@conjungi.com	Seattle, WA USA
CREDO NET	Raptor and security consulting	info@credo.net	22941 Triton Way Suite 241 Laguna Hills, CA USA (888) 88-CREDO

Company	Products/ Services	E-mail	Contact Information
CyberCorp	NetGuard Control Center	amuse@ cyberservices.com	2934 West Royal Lane Suite 3136 Irving, TX 75063 USA (972) 738-6916
Cypress Systems	Raptor	rmck	P.O. Box 9070 McLean, VA 22101 USA (703) 273-2150
Data General	Cybershield and Raptor	sense@dg.com	4400 Computer Drive Westboro, MA 01580 USA (800) 4DG-OPEN
Decision-Science Applications Applications	BorderWare FireWall-1 Sidewinder and more	infosec@dsava.com	1110 N. Glebe Rd., Suite 400 Arlington, VA 22201 USA (703) 875-9600 or 243-2500
Deerfield Communications	WinGate Instant Internet	info@deerfield.com	(517) 732-8856
DFC International Ltd.	IBM Firewall	sales@dfc.com	52 Mowatt Court Thornhill, Ontario L3T 6V5 Tel: (905) 731-6449
Digital Pathways UK	Sidewinder	-	-
Dimension Data Security	Firewall-1 and security products	mouritz@ddsecurity. co.za	158 Jan Smuts Ave. Rosebank P.O. Box 3234 Parklands 2121 South Africa Tel: +27 (0)11-283-5116
DNS Telecom	SecureNet and SecurSite, Watchguard and others	preynes@dnstele com.fr	Immeuble La Fayette 2 place des vosges 92051 Paris la Difense 5 France Tel: +33 (0)1 43 34 10 17
Dynavar Networking	Ascend, Cisco PIX and many others	sales@dynavar.com	#300, 1550 - 5th Street SW Calgary, Alberta, Canada T2R 1K3 Tel: (403) 571-5000

Company	Products/ Services	E-mail	Contact Information
East Coast Software	NetGuard Control Center and security consulting	infotec@eastcoastsw. com.au	PO Box 6494 St Kilda Road Central, Melbourne, Victoria 3004 AUS. Tel: 61-3-9821-4848
Electric Mail	Firewall-1 and Internet products	info@elmail.co.uk	Merlin Place, Milton Road Cambridge United Kingdom Tel: +44 (0) 1223 501 333
EMJ America	AFS 2000, BorderWare and others	mrkusa@emji.net	1434 Farrington Road Apex, NC 27502 USA (800) 548-2319
Enstar Networking	Firewall-1 and security consulting	baustin@enstar.com	8304 Esters Blvd. Suite 840 Dallas, TX 75063 USA (800) 367-4254
Enterprise System Solutions	BorderWare	-	-
FishNet Consulting Services	Firewall-1, others, and security consulting	info@kcfishnet.com	7007 College Blvd. Suite 450 Overland Park, KS 66211 USA (913) 498-0711
Garrison Technologies	Security consulting, firewalls, audits, etc.	sales@garrison.com	100 Congress Ave. Suite 2100 Austin, TX 78701 USA (512) 302-0882
GearSource	NetGuard Control Center PIX	sales@GearSource. com	5015 Victor Street Dallas, TX 75214 USA (214) 821-7909
Global Data Systems	Firewalls and security	glasane@gdsconnect. com	(781) 740-8818
Global Technology Associates	GTA firewalls and security services	david@globaltech. co.uk	71 Portland Road Worthing West Sussex BN11 1QG England Tel: 44 (0) 1903 20 51 51

Company	Products/ Services	E-mail	Contact Information
Graphics Computer Systems	Firewall-1 and security services	sales@gcs.com.au	97 Highbury Road Burwood, Victoria Australia 3125 Tel: +61 3 9888 8522
Haystack Labs now owned by Network Associates	Stalker Intrusion detection system	info@haystack.com	10713 RR620N, Suite 521 Austin, TX 78726 USA (512) 918-3555
Herve Schauer Consultants	HSC GateKeeper	info@hsc.fr	142, rue de Rivoli 75039 Paris Cedex 01 France Tel: +33 (1) 46.38.89.90
HomeCom Internet Security Services	Firewall and security sales and consulting	security@homecom. com	1900 Gallows Road Vienna, VA 22182 USA (703) 847-1702
IConNet	Internet in a Rack (IR) Network hardware and software	info@iconnet.net	-
Inflo Communications Limited	Raptor firewall and others	sales@inflo.co.uk	Mountcharles Road Donegal Town Co. Donegal Ireland Tel: +353 73 23111
Ingress Consulting Group	BorderWare and others	sales@nohackers.com	60 Guild Street Norwood, MA 02062 USA (888) INGRESS
Integralis UK	MIMEsweeper	msw.support@ integralis.co.uk	U.K. +44 (0) 1734 306060
Integralis USA		info@us.integralis. com	US (206) 889-5841
Intercede Ltd.	MilkyWay SecureIT	sales@intercede.co.uk	1 Castle Street, Hinckley, Leicestershire LE10 1DA UK Tel: +44 (0) 1455 250 266
INTERNET GmbH	BorderWare consulting	Ingmar Schraub	Am Burgacker 23 D-69488 Birkenau Germany Tel: +49-6201-3999-59
Jerboa	Independent security and firewall consulting	info@jerboa.com	Box 382648 Cambridge, MA 02238 (617) 492-8084

Company	Products/ Services	E-mail	Contact Information
Kerna Commuications Ltd.	Security consultants, firewall installation and support	sales@kerna.ie	3 Arbourfield Terrace, Dundrum, Dublin 14 Ireland Tel: +353-1-2964396
The Knowledge Group	VCS Firewall and Security products	sales@ktgroup.co.uk	Concorde Road Patchway, Bristol UK Tel: +44 (0) 117 900 7500
LANhouse Communications	Ascend, Centri Firewall, Gauntlet and security consulting	sales@lanhouse.com	510 King Street East Suite 202 Toronto, Ontario, Canada M5A 1M1 Tel: (416) 367-2300
LURHQ Corporation	Security consulting, firewalls, Web server security	info@lurhq.com	P.O. Box 2861 Conway, SC 29526 USA (843) 347-1075
Madison Technology Group	Security/FW design & implementation	Steveng@microlan.com	331 Madison Ave. 6th Floor NYC, NY 10017 USA (212) 883-1000
Master Software Technology	AltaVista and CS consulting	sales@masteredge.com	92 Montvale Ave. Stoneham, MA 02180 USA (617) 438-8330
media communications eur ab	Gauntlet security consulting	neil@medcom.se	Box 1144 111 81 stockholm, Sweden Tel: +46.708.432224 (GSM)
Mergent International	Gauntlet security consulting	info@mergent.com	(800) 688-1199
Midwest Systems	Gauntlet Sidewinder VAR	lschwanke@midwest-sys.com	2800 Southcross Dr. West Burnsville, MN 55306 USA (612) 894-4020
MPS Ltd.	M>Wall and security consulting	johnt@mpsuk.com	The Manor Stables Great Somerford Nr Chippenham Wiltshire SN15 5EH England Tel: +44 (0) 1249 721414

Company	Products/ Services	E-mail	Contact Information
NetGuard	NetGuard Control Center	solutions@ntguard. com	11350 Random Hill Road Suite 750 Fairfax, VA 22030 USA (703) 359-8150
NetPartners Internet Solutions	WebSENSE, Firewall-1, Raptor, and others	sales@netpart.com	9665 Chesapeake Dr. Suite 350 San Diego, CA 92123 USA (800) 723-1166 or (619) 505-3020
Netrex	Secure Internet Solutions Firewall-1	info@netrex.com	3000 Town Center Suite 1100 Southfield, MI 48075 USA (800) 3.NETREX
Network Associates	Gauntlet and many security products	contacts	3965 Freedom Circle Santa Clara, CA 95054 USA (408) 988-3832
Network Security	Firewall-1, NetScreen and others	info@nsec.net	369 River Road North Tonawanda, NY 14120 USA (716) 692-8183
Obtuse Systems	Juniper	info@obtuse.com	Alberta, Canada
Breakwater Security Associates	Many firewalls and security consulting	info@breakwater.net	(206) 770-0700
Orbis Internet	Sidewinder and security consulting	dan@orbis.net	475 Cleveland Ave. North Suite 222 St. Paul, MN 55104 USA (612) 603-9030
Qualix	Firewall-1 and security products	qdirect@qualix.com	177 Bovet Road, 2nd Floor San Mateo, CA 94402 USA (650) 572-0200
Racal Airtech Ltd	Raptor Security services	Sohbat Ali	Meadow View House Long Crendon, Aylesbury Buckinghamshire, UK HP18 9EQ Tel: 01844 201800

Company	Products/ Services	E-mail	Contact Information
Racal Gaurdata	Raptor Security services	Sohbat Ali	480 Spring Park Place Suite 900 Herndon, VA 22070 USA (703) 471-0892
Reese Web	Raptor	pp001261@ interramp.com	Rocky Point Harbour 3309 Diamond Knot Circle Tampa, FL 33607 USA (813) 286-7065
Sandman Security of Smoke N' Mirrors Inc	Firewall-1 Raptor and others	Ben Taylor	1165 Herndon Pkwy. Suite 200 Herndon, VA 20170 USA (703) 318-1440
Sea Change Pacific Region	BorderWare	jalsop@seachange. com michael@seawest	5159 Beckton Road Victoria, British Columbia V8Y 2C2 (604) 658-5448
Sea Change Europe Ltd	BorderWare	jalsop@seachange.com peter@sea-europe.co.uk	470 London Road Slough, Berks SL3 8QY UK Tel: 44-1753-581800
Secure Network Systems	Many firewalls and security and network consulting	info@blanket.com	Lawrence, Kansas USA
SecureXpert Labs FSC Internet Corp	Security consulting and information FireWall-1 and others	security@securexpert.com	-
Serverware Group plc	iWay-One	sale@serverwr.de.mon. co.uk	Tel: (44) 1732-464624
Sherwood Data Systems Ltd	Karl Bridge/Karl Brouter	sales@gbnet.com	High Wycombe, UK Tel: +44 (0) 1494 464264
Silicon Graphics	Gauntlet and Security	Sales	39001 West 12 Mile Rd. Farmington, MI 48331 USA (800) 800-7441
Siemens Nixdorf	TrustedWeb	info@trustedweb.com	Fitzwilliam Court Leeson Close Dublin 2, Ireland

Company	Products/ Services	E-mail	Contact Information
SkyNet Czech Republic	Gauntlet	Roman.Paklik@ SkyNet.CZ	Kabatnikova 5 602 00 Brno Czech Republic Tel: +420 5 41 24 59 79
SMC Electronic Commerce Ltd	Gauntlet, many other FWs, and security consulting	info@smcgroup.co.za	52 Wierda Rd West Wierda Vally, Sandton South Africa Tel: +27 11 2694005
Softway Pty Ltd	Gauntlet and security consulting	enquiries@softway. com.au	P.O. Box 305 Strawberry Hills, NSW 2012 Australia Tel: +61 2 9698-2322
Stallion Ltd.	Firewall-1 and security services	stallion@stallion.ee	Mustamae tee 55, Tallinn 10621, Estonia Tel: +372 6 567720
Stonesoft Corporation	Stonebeat and Firewall-1	info@stone.fi	Taivalm=E4ki 9 FIN-02200 Espoo, Finland Tel: +358 9 476711 Tel: +358 9 4767 1282
StorageTek Network	ATM, NCF, BorderGuard	webmaster@network.com	Tel: (800) NET INFO
Sun Tzu Security	Firewalls and security consulting	info@suntzu.net	Tel: (414) 289-0966
Symbolic	COOL-FIRE and security services	mt@symbolic.it	Viale Mentana 29 I-43100 Parma, Italy Tel: +39 521 776180
Technology Management Systems	BlackHole	tmsinc@erols.com	Vienna, VA 22181 USA Tel: (703) 768-3139
Technology Transition Services	Fort Knox Firewall and security consulting	sales@techtranserv.com	100 Blue Run Rd. Indianola, PA 15051 USA
Trident Data Systems	SunScreen Firewall-1 and security consulting	Anthony Dinga (east) Bob Hermann (west) Charlie Johnson (midwest)	5933 W. Century Blvd. Suite 700 Los Angeles, CA 90045 USA Tel: (310) 645-6483

Company	Products/ Services	E-mail	Contact Information
Tripcom Systems	Firewall-1 and Internet consulting	Adam Horwitz	Naperville, IL USA Tel: (708) 778-9531
Trusted Information Systems	Gauntlet	tis@tis.com (US) info@eu.tis.com (non-US)	Tel: (301 854-6889 or (410) 442-1673
Trusted Network Solutions	Gauntlet and security consulting	-	Johannesburg, South Africa
UNIXPAC Australia	Raptor and network consulting	info@unixpac.com.au	Cremorne, Australia Tel: (02) 9953 8366 or 1 800 022 137
Uunet	Raptor and others security consulting	info@uu,net	3060 Willliams Drive Fairfax, VA 22031 USA (800) 488-6383 or (703) 206-5600
Vanstar	All major security products and consulting	Jrecor@vanstar.com	30800 Telegraph Rd. Suite 1850 Bingham Farms, MI 48312 USA (810) 540-6493
We Connect People Inc.	Security FWs, Internet consulting and more	sales@wcpinc.com	California, USA (408) 421-0857
WheelGroup	NetRanger/NetSonar, intrusion detection and other security products	sales@wheelgroup.com	13750 San Pedro Suite 670 San Antonio, TX 78232 USA (210) 494-3383
X + Open Systems Pty Ltd	Security FWs and network services	info@xplus.com.au	P.O. Box 6456 Shoppingworld North Sydney, NSW 2059 AU Tel: +61 2 9957 6152
Zeuros Limited	Raptor and network services	les@zeuros.co.uk	Tudor Barn, Frog Lane Rotherwick, Hampshire, RG27 9BE, UK Tel: 44 (0) 1256 760081
ZONEOFTRUST.COM	Security products, FWs and services	info@zoneoftrust.com	22941 Triton Way 2nd Flr. Laguna Hills, CA 92653 USA (714) 859-0196

Appendix 6.C: Public Domain, Shareware, etc.

- **Drawbridge**
  Available at *net.tamu.edu*

- **Freestone by SOS Corporation**
  Freestone is an application gateway firewall package, a genetic derivative of *Brimstone* produced by *SOS Corporation*. Freestone can be retrieved from the *Columbia, SOS*, and *COAST* FTP sites

- **fwtk - firewall toolkit**
  Available from ftp.tis.com Look in /pub/firewalls and /pub/firewalls/toolkit for documentation and toolkit.

- **ISS**
  Internet Security Scanner is an auditing package that checks domains and nodes searching for well-known vulnerabilities and generating a log for the administrator to take corrective measures. For information, history, and the commercial versions by the originator, visit: *www.iss.net*. For the publicly available version, I have no current ftp site, but you might try various search engines.

- **Mediator One**
  Non-commercial shareware firewall.

- **router-config tool**
  A set of KornShell scripts (known to run cleanly on UnixWare and Solaris, and with very minor tweeking on SGI's but doesn't run with pd-ksh) to build the very complex router configurations needed for high-quality packet-filtering firewalls (only generates configs for Cisco, though there are facilities for adding other router types). Software is available from the *Freebird Archive.*

- **SOCKS**
  The SOCKS package, developed by David Koplas and Ying Da Lee. Available by ftp from ftp.nec.com. Also see: *www.socks.nec.com*

*The source of these appendices is *www.waterw.com/~manowar/vendor.html*. Please check this web site for the latest information.

Chapter 7
Security Policy

Security concerns have heightened in recent years. News stories about viruses and computer fraud dominate. Information technology (IT) managers have to decide how to protect information and computer technology.

In developing a security policy, you must consider not only actual security threats but also the security perceptions of the public. For example, although it is in fact much safer to provide a credit card number over the Internet to a legitimate company than to give it to an unscrupulous employee in a face-to-face transaction, many people express concern about providing credit card numbers over the Internet. Not responding to the public's concerns may result in significant financial loss.

As a manager you face several trade-offs concerning security management. While some may be quantified, others—such as determining the organization's strategic direction—cannot. That's why both the IT and the human resources departments should be considered in formulating a security plan.

Without an adequate security policy, your organization is vulnerable to many threats, including:

- Theft of both electronic and physical resources, including data

- Unauthorized modification of data

- Fraud and other illegal activities

- Disclosure of confidential and proprietary information

- Unintentional errors caused by carelessness

- Intentional sabotage caused by current or former disgruntled employees

- Spying or sabotage by competitors
- Inability to continue business after an emergency or disaster

Managing Computer Security

In formulating a policy you must first ask yourself some questions:

1. What resources need to be protected?
2. Against whom must we protect our system?
3. How much can we spend to protect the system?
4. What benefits will we derive from the expenditure? Is the benefit worth the cost?
5. What happens if security is compromised? How will we respond?
6. What are our contingency plans?

Private, confidential, proprietary data is typically one important resource you want to protect. Otherwise, your financial assets might be compromised. Other valuable resources include CPU processing cycles or computer time. While attackers are typically interested in obtaining access to confidential data, some may simply want to deny legitimate users access to computer facilities.

Even information not likely to be valuable to anyone else should be protected. Hackers often steal or destroy data simply because it's there. They may also delete or destroy files in an attempt to cover up illegal activity.

When you're calculating the cost of security precautions, consider not only the direct but also the indirect costs. Direct costs may be for equipment, installation, and training. Indirect costs include the effects on morale and productivity.

It's prudent to recognize that increasing security decreases convenience. Employees and others, such as customers and suppliers, may resent the inconvenience. Too much security may be just as detrimental as too little; the goal is an optimal equilibrium.

In spite of precautions, security will eventually be compromised. The steps you take to recover from such a breach may mean the difference between success and failure in your business. Think about such questions as the following:

- What will be the financial impact of a security breach?
- Do you have enough insurance?
- What may be the legal consequences of a breach?
- How will lost data, information, or assets be recovered?
- How will the breach affect employees, suppliers, or customers?
- How can similar events be prevented in the future?

Creating the Policy and the Plan

The purpose of a security *plan* is to assign accountability. The security *policy* should define what is and is not acceptable.

The plan should clearly specify the penalties for unacceptable behavior. How will you reprimand violators inside the organization? How will you deal with violators outside? What type of civil or criminal action might you take?

The security policy should be integrated with your company's other policies and plans. For example, think about the internal control structure. Plan for contingencies. Make sure all your plans comply with the laws.

The role of the information systems department should be specified in the policy document. The department should be responsible for, among other things, ensuring that security personnel are adequately trained and properly qualified. IS security personnel should be able to assist other departments with their security needs. Other responsibilities of security personnel might include:

- Assisting in acquiring hardware or operating systems
- Managing security of the communications networks
- Establishing standards for remote access
- Installing and maintaining virus detection software
- Selecting cryptographic techniques and keys
- Backing up critical data
- Evaluating and approving IS-related contracts

The Security Policy

The security *policy* should be a broad statement that guides personnel and departments in achieving certain goals. It should be concise and easy to read. It should not specify actions. The purpose of the security policy is not to educate or train individuals. That should be provided for in manuals and seminars.

The security policy, then, is written at a broad organizational level. The standards, guidelines, and procedures go into supporting documents. Some questions the policy should answer are:

- Why is it important to have a security policy?
- What is the meaning of data integrity?
- Why must data integrity be maintained?
- Why should data be kept confidential?
- What are the consequences to the organization if data is unavailable or compromised?

Standards, Guidelines, and Procedures

Standards, guidelines, and procedures provide the guidance the members of your organization need to realize the goals defined in the policy document. They give people clear instructions on how to meet organizational goals. *Standards* and *guidelines* specify the technologies and methodologies that may be used; *procedures* offer more detailed guidance to achieve particular security objectives.

All three should be published in handbooks, regulations, or manuals, both physical and electronic, as on the corporate Intranet or on CD-ROM. Providing the information in an electronic format has several advantages, among them easy access. It also makes it easier for you to keep the information current.

The purpose of *standards* is to specify a uniform set of technologies or procedures. Standards are typically mandatory; users may not exercise their own discretion in the areas they cover.

Guidelines, on the other hand, are provided because it's not always possible, appropriate, or cost-effective to impose standards. Guidelines give users some latitude in meeting goals. Guidelines are used to ensure, for example, that specific security measures are not overlooked. Guidelines inherently recognize that security measures may be correctly implemented in more than one way.

Procedures offer step-by-step guidance in adhering to standards and guidelines.

Buy-in

If you want your security policy to be effective, solicit participation from across the organization, both individuals and departments. Senior management's support is essential. You must provide the resources, financial and otherwise, to implement the policy adequately.

At the same time, users are far more likely to accept security policy, guidelines, and procedures if they had input in creating them. Their participation will help you create a better policy plan. The specialized knowledge each brings will result in a superior document.

Set up a senior management committee (the Information Security Management Committee) with authority to issue and amend the security policy. Make sure that people get from committee approval for any exceptions to the security policy.

Scope

Your computer security policy should apply to all facilities and locations of the company. The same set of standards should be enforced throughout the company. While it's essential that security standards be applied consistently, they should be flexible enough to be used in a variety of situations.

Your security policies should encompass all types of computer systems, including stand-alone PCs, LANs, WANs, the Internet, and the Intranet. They should cover all types of data transmission, including e-mail, FTP, and fax.

Risk Analysis and Management

Computer security planning is an integral part of your organization's overall risk management strategy. Each individual's and each department's responsibility should be clearly identified in the security plan, which should be updated regularly to meet changes in technology or circumstances.

You must therefore do a thorough risk analysis. Computer security risks fall into five major categories:

1. Destruction of data or equipment

2. Theft of data or equipment

3. Malfunction of equipment or bugs in software

4. Modification of data

5. Disclosure of data

The cause of risk may be:

- Intentional attack
- Unintentional or accidental loss
- Environmental threat

Intentional threat comes from computer criminals and disgruntled employees setting out to defraud, sabotage, alter data, or steal equipment or data. *Unintentional* loss may result from computer users who are careless. *Accidental* loss may be due to equipment malfunction. *Environmental* threats include fires, floods, earthquakes, lightning, and power outages. An effective security plan must cover all these threats.

Take out insurance policies to cover such risks as theft, fraud, intentional destruction, and forgery. Don't forget business interruption insurance, which covers lost profits and additional expenses during downtime.

Your risk analysis should take into account not only the security but also the reliability of your system; this can be compromised by errors, failures, and faults. An *error* is a deviation from expectations. Some errors are acceptable because they can be overcome; others are simply unacceptable. An unacceptable error is a *failure.* If the failure can have serious consequences, it's considered a *critical failure.* A *fault* is a condition that results in a failure.

It's important to note, however, that system reliability is conceptually distinct from system security. The purpose of computer system security is to protect against intentional misuse. System security doesn't really consider malfunctions or bugs unless they will allow a perpetrator to breach security. Still, improving one factor will typically enhance the effects of the other. That's why both security and reliability should be considered in managing risk.

The Security Administrator

The security administrator is responsible for customizing security policies and standards to the organization and for the planning, execution, and maintenance of the computer security system. The administrator should regularly interact with other departments to learn of their changing needs. Both technical computer knowledge and management skills are therefore necessary attributes for the security administrator, as well as a thorough understanding of the organization's internal control structure.

Specific aspects of an organization, such as its size and inherent risks, have to be taken into account in setting up the security administration department. The department must ensure the information systems data is reliable and accurate. Members of the department should keep abreast of organizational requirements in dynamic environments to keep the security system efficient while monitoring staff to ensure compliance with policies. It is particularly important for you to have in place specific procedures for hiring and recruiting staff for this department (see Chapter 5).

The Human Factor

Typically, security systems depend more on people and their attitudes toward security than on the latest technology. Typically, too, the greatest security threat in an organization comes not from outsiders but from insiders. Personnel incompetence, indifference, and negligence are likely to cause more harm than sabotage or intentional acts by unauthorized hackers.

Security policies and procedures often conflict with people's ideas of good manners. Trusting others and sharing things with them is viewed positively. Security policies, on the other hand, require that you distrust others and not share information. For example, it's normally considered polite to hold a door open for someone behind you. However, in a restricted area, such politeness will result in a security breach. Similarly, sharing user IDs or passwords may allow an unauthorized individual to access sensitive information.

Psychological Factors[1]

To make sure the people in your company accept the security policy, M.E. Kabay, director of education for the National Computer Security Association, recommends:

- Before attempting to implement policies and procedures, build up a consistent view of information security among your colleagues.

- Introduce security policies over time, don't rush them into place.

---

[1]M.E. Kabay, "Psycho-Social Factors in the Implementation of Information Security Policy," National Computer Security Association (see *http://nsi.org/*).

- Present case studies to help get people ready to accept security requirements.
- Give your people many realistic examples of security requirements and breaches.
- Inspire a commitment to security rather than merely describing it.
- Emphasize improvement effects rather than failure reduction.
- Explore the current beliefs of employees and managers.
- Don't portray computer crime with any positive images or words.
- Praise comments that are critical of computer crime or that support the security policies.
- Challenge rather than ignore employees who dismiss security concerns or flout the regulations.
- Identify the senior executives most likely to set a positive tone for security training.
- Immediately couple frightening consequences with effective and achievable security measures.
- Present objections to a proposal and offer counter-arguments rather than giving a one-sided diatribe.
- Make sure repeated novel reminders of security issues are part of your security awareness program.
- Include small gifts in your security awareness program.
- Find a charismatic leader to help generate enthusiasm for better security.
- Encourage specific employees to take on public responsibility for information security within their work groups.
- Rotate the security role periodically.
- Incorporate into your security training information on how to tell when someone may be engaging in computer crime.
- Build a corporate culture that rewards responsible behavior such as reporting security violations.
- Develop clearly written security policies and procedures.
- Be sure your security procedures make it easy to act in accordance with security policy.

- Emphasize the seriousness of failing to act in accordance with security policies and procedures.
- Enforce standards of security so that employees will later follow the standards more rigorously.
- Create a working environment in which employees are respected; this is more conducive to good security than one that devalues and abuses them.
- Have security supervisors get to know the staff.
- Encourage social activities in the office.
- Pay special attention to social "outliers" during training programs.
- Monitor compliance closely to security requirements.
- Work with the outliers to resist the herd's anti-security bias.
- Before discussing security at a meeting, have one-on-one discussions with participants.
- Remain impartial; encourage open debate in security meetings.
- Bring in experts from the outside when faced with groupthink.
- Meet again after a consensus has been built and play devil's advocate.

Seminars

The importance of computer security must be instilled in all employees. Direct communication is typically more effective at persuading individuals than mass media like videos or books. Personalized messages stimulate thought and are likely to be more persuasive. An excellent way to both indoctrinate new employees and update the skills of current employees is to periodically schedule security seminars. Security professionals can communicate your company's rules and procedures at these seminars, as well as answer questions and address the security needs of employees.

Assign senior executives who are liked and respected to lead the seminars. A speaker's attractiveness and social status have an immediate effect on the audience. For a few days, the speaker's personal characteristics will continue to influence the audience, though the effect typically declines with the passage of time till only the message remains with the audience. The speaker should understand security issues and honestly believe in the policies he or she is advocating.

In trying to persuade employees, it's useful to present a balanced view, especially when trying to convince those who initially disagree with your policy. By presenting both sides of the argument you show your audience that you understand their perspective and have sound reasons for your own.

Other Communication Channels

Lecturing employees for a few hours per year, however, is unlikely to lead to improved security by itself. People need time to accept and acclimate to change; that's why new security policies should typically be phased in over time.

Repetition of the security message is helpful in building support for security policies. Security awareness may be enhanced with mugs, posters, and newsletters. Ongoing activities will yield better results than occasional training seminars alone, necessary though these are.

Videos and case studies containing examples of security breaches can have a beneficial effect. Exposing individuals to different security scenarios helps increase their awareness of security issues. Humans are not good intuitive statisticians. Intuitive human judgment is often prone to bias. Judgment is easily distorted when individuals tend to rely on small samples, easily available data, and personal anecdotal experience.

The use of questionnaires, focus groups, and interviews, may serve several purposes. They can help you obtain useful information about employees. They may also help to modify employee's beliefs, leading to a greater commitment to security. If you publicly support enhanced security, employees will change their perceptions and be more committed to security. When they take responsibility openly, their commitment to the task increases.

Behavior Modification

You can modify employee behavior by rewarding employees who support and punishing employees who violate security policies. The reward may be as simple as verbal praise. The punishment may be a simple verbal warning, disciplinary action, or even removal from the job. Employees who flagrantly violate security policies should certainly hear about it.

The use of fear to change the attitudes of employees works only in certain situations. Too much fear about catastrophic consequences is likely to result in employees rejecting the message. When you tell employees about catastrophic consequences, also show them how to counter threats.

Account Administration

New users are continually being added to your system while old users must be deleted. Establish a written procedure for requesting, creating, maintaining, and closing user accounts. The purpose of account administration is to ensure that:

- The user is authorized.
- The user has access privileges appropriate to the job.
- The user is not engaged in unauthorized activities.
- Information about the user is current.

The user's supervisor should initiate the account creation process by requesting an account from the systems manager. The request should specify access level and the applications to which the user should have access. The approval of an applications manager may be required before the systems manager grants access to a particular application.

The user access level should be part of the account profile. Specific applications may have built-in access controls or may rely on third-party software for access control. The systems manager must ensure that a user's access is consistent with the request from the supervisor.

On being issued the user account and password, employees should undergo security training. At the very least, users should be provided with the written rules and guidelines and be required to sign an "account assignment" document indicating their understanding of those rules and guidelines. The document may be used to discipline or even prosecute users who violate them.

There are two techniques for creating user account IDs. The ID could be for a specific job title (SALESREP4) or for a specific employee (JACK_BLACK). From an auditing perspective, job title IDs simplify the process. However, if the account ID is for a specific job title, you'll need controls to ensure that the password is changed as soon as the employee changes jobs or leaves.

The user's supervisor should notify the systems and applications managers when a user is reassigned or the account is no longer required. The personnel department should also be required to notify those managers when there's a change in personnel or duties.

Access level privileges change. The change might be temporary or permanent. An employee may be temporarily performing the duties of another employee who is sick or on vacation. An employee may also be permanently assigned a different function or transferred to another department.

When an employee takes on additional duties during the absence of another employee, take care to ensure that he or she is not performing incompatible duties. From a control perspective, no one should be in a position to perpetrate an irregularity and cover it up in the normal course of the day. Temporary access privileges should also be removed as soon as they are no longer needed.

User accounts should be reviewed regularly to help detect unauthorized or illegal activities. The review may be of a sample of user accounts or the entire system. The level of access of each user should also be reviewed. Make sure that all new accounts have supervisory approval, and that the level of access granted is warranted by the job responsibilities.

Check that the accounts of all personnel who left the organization or were reassigned were properly closed, comparing data from the personnel department and the system manager's records.

Examine account records to assure that all users signed a statement acknowledging their understanding of rules and guidelines and that they have taken security awareness training.

For certain functions, periodic screening checks of personnel may be warranted. For example, an individual living a lifestyle considerably in excess of income is a red flag; it may be the fruit of fraudulent activity. The individual may be stealing corporate assets or giving competitors proprietary information.

Review the controls over account management during an audit and check compliance with controls. Just because a control exists doesn't mean users are actually following it.

One important control we have already mentioned is segregation of duties so that the employee cannot commit and conceal an illegal activity in the normal course of duties. Mandating that employees take vacations is also important from a security perspective. Some fraudulent activities require the perpetrators to take certain actions on a regular basis to prevent the fraud from being discovered.

In addition to mandatory vacations, you may want to rotate job assignments periodically. This serves the same purpose: It prevents a perpetrator from covering up illegal activities. Rotating job assignments has other benefits: When several individuals are trained to perform a single function, the organization is not excessively dependent on any single employee.

Conclusion

The primary benefit of the computer security policy is to prevent or minimize the loss of assets or resources due to a security breach. The document also provides a decision-making framework for purchasing software and hardware. It gives guidelines for steps to take after a security breach to prevent further breaches or losses.

A formal risk assessment should be part of the document. Assets to be protected, threats to those assets, and safeguards for those assets should be analyzed.

The rights and obligations of the users should be specified, along with rules for account use. Conditions that apply to personal users as well as public access accounts should be detailed. The document should also include criteria of acceptability of user software along with data access and use policies.

Users should be specifically warned against disclosing their passwords or other information that could potentially threaten the computer system. Privacy policies, including those applying to disclosure of confidential information to third parties, should be prominent, with special attention to user privacy, including conditions when the company may access a user's files.

The security policy should state what will happen if there is a security breach. It should answer questions like:

- If a security breach is in progress, who should be notified, and how?
- What audit trail must be maintained? What log files should be kept?
- How will the affected computer system or network be identified and isolated?
- What are the legal ramifications of entrapment? When must security officers identify themselves?
- How will violators be punished?
- When will law enforcement authorities be notified?
- How will the organization recover from a security breach?

Appendix 7.A: Sources of Information Security Policies

You can find prewritten information security policies at the Web site for Baseline Software, Inc. (*http://www.baselinesoft.com/*). You may want to use Baseline as a starting point, customizing as needed.

Information Security Policies Made Easy Version 7 (7th edition) by Charles Cresson Wood, October 31, 1999, sets out some 840 policies, each with an explanation. The book comes with a CD-ROM containing files that may be edited in various word processing programs. It may be accessed at *www.baselinesoft.com*. Topics covered include:

- Computer emergency response teams
- Computer viruses
- Contingency planning
- Data classification
- Digital signatures
- Electronic commerce
- Electronic mail
- Employee surveillance
- Encryption
- Firewalls
- Internet
- Intranets
- Local area networks
- Logging controls
- Microcomputers
- Outsourcing security functions
- Password selection
- Portable computers
- Privacy issues
- Telecommuting
- Telephone systems
- User training
- Web pages

Appendix 7.B: Sample Computer Policy

Georgia Institute of Technology's Computer and Network Usage Policy
(Available at *www.business.gatech.edu/depts/andits/internal.htm*)

Preface
Respect for intellectual labor and creativity is vital to academic discourse and enterprise. This principle applies to works of all authors and publishers in all media. It encompasses respect for the right to acknowledgment, the right to privacy, and the right to determine the form, manner, and terms of publication and distribution. Because electronic information is volatile and easily reproduced, respect for the work and personal expression of others is especially critical in computer environments. Violations of authorial integrity, including plagiarism, invasion of privacy, unauthorized access, and trade secret and copyright violations, may be grounds for sanctions against members of the academic community. The EDUCOM Code.

1. BACKGROUND AND PURPOSE
This document constitutes an Institute-wide policy intended to allow for the proper use of all Georgia Tech computing and network resources, effective protection of individual users, equitable access, and proper management of those resources. This should be taken in the broadest possible sense. This policy applies to Georgia Tech network usage even in situations where it would not apply to the computer(s) in use. These guidelines are intended to supplement, not replace, all existing laws, regulations, agreements, and contracts which currently apply to these services.

Campus units that operate their own computers or networks may add, with the approval of the unit head, individual guidelines which supplement, but do not relax, this policy. In such cases, the unit should inform their users and the Information Resources Security Coordinator in OIT prior to implementation.

Access to networks and computer systems owned or operated by Georgia Tech imposes certain responsibilities and obligations and is granted subject to Institute policies and local, state, and federal laws. Appropriate use should always be legal, ethical, reflect academic honesty, reflect community standards, and show restraint in the consumption of shared resources. It should demonstrate respect for intellectual property; ownership of data; system security mechanisms; and individuals rights to privacy and to freedom from intimidation, harassment, and unwarranted annoyance. Appropriate use of computing and networking resources includes instruction; independent study; authorized research; independent research; communications; and official work of the offices, units, recognized student and campus organizations, and agencies of the Institute.

2. DEFINITIONS

2.1. Authorized use

Authorized use of Georgia Tech-owned or operated computing and network resources is use consistent with the education, research, and service mission of the Institute, and consistent with this policy.

2.2. Authorized users

Authorized users are: (1) current faculty, staff, and students of the Institute; (2) anyone connecting to a public information service (see section 6.5); (3) others whose access furthers the mission of the Institute and whose usage does not interfere with other users' access to resources. The policy Access by External Entities to Institute Information Technology Resources (OIT, 11/3/93, and any subsequent revisions) may apply. In addition, a user must be specifically authorized to use a particular computing or network resource by the campus unit responsible for operating the resource.

3. INDIVIDUAL PRIVILEGES

It is the following individual privileges, all of which are currently existent at Georgia Tech, that empower each of us to be productive members of the campus community. It must be understood that privileges are conditioned upon acceptance of the accompanying responsibilities.

3.1. Privacy

To the greatest extent possible in a public setting we want to preserve the individual's privacy. Electronic and other technological methods must not be used to infringe upon privacy. However, users must recognize that Georgia Tech computer systems and networks are public and subject to the Georgia Open Records Act. Users, thus, utilize such systems at their own risk.

3.2. Freedom of expression

The constitutional right to freedom of speech applies to all members of the campus no matter the medium used.

3.3. Ownership of intellectual works

People creating intellectual works using Georgia Tech computers or networks, including but not limited to software, should consult Determination of Rights and Equities in Intellectual Property (Board of Regents Policy Manual, section 603.03, 2/2/94 and any subsequent revisions), and related Georgia Tech policies.

3.4. Freedom from harassment and undesired information

All members of the campus have the right not to be harassed by computer or network usage by others. (See 4.1.3.)

4. INDIVIDUAL RESPONSIBILITIES

Just as certain privileges are given to each member of the campus community, each of us is held accountable for our actions as a condition of continued membership in the community. The interplay of privileges and responsibilities within each individual situation and across campus engenders the trust and intellectual freedom that form the heart of our community. This trust and freedom are grounded on each person's developing the skills necessary to be an active and contributing member of the community. These skills include an awareness and knowledge about information and the technology used to process, store, and transmit it.

4.1. Common courtesy and respect for rights of others

You are responsible to all other members of the campus community in many ways, including to respect and value the rights of privacy for all, to recognize and respect the diversity of the population and opinion in the community, to behave ethically, and to comply with all legal restrictions regarding the use of information that is the property of others.

4.1.1. Privacy of information

Files of personal information, including programs, no matter on what medium they are stored or transmitted, may be subject to the Georgia Open Records Act if stored on Georgia Tech's computers. That fact notwithstanding, no one should look at, copy, alter, or destroy anyone elses personal files without explicit permission (unless authorized or required to do so by law or regulation). Simply being able to access a file or other information does not imply permission to do so.

Similarly, no one should connect to a host on the network without advance permission in some form. People and organizations link computers to the network for numerous different reasons, and many consider unwelcome connects to be attempts to invade their privacy or compromise their security.

4.1.2. Intellectual property

You are responsible for recognizing (attributing) and honoring the intellectual property rights of others.

4.1.3. Harassment

No member of the community may, under any circumstances, use Georgia Tech's computers or networks to libel, slander, or harass any other person.

The following shall constitute Computer Harassment: (1) Intentionally using the computer to annoy, harass, terrify, intimidate, threaten, offend or bother another person by conveying obscene language, pictures, or other materials or threats of bodily harm to the recipient or the recipient's immediate family; (2) Intentionally using the computer to contact another person repeatedly with the intent to annoy, harass, or bother, whether or not any actual message is communicated, and/or where no purpose of legitimate communication exists, and where the recipient has expressed a desire for the communication to cease; (3) Intentionally using the computer to contact another person repeatedly regarding a matter for which one does not have a legal right to communicate, once the recipient has provided reasonable notice that he or she desires such communication to cease (such as debt collection); (4) Intentionally using the computer to disrupt or damage the academic, research, administrative, or related pursuits of another; (5) Intentionally using the computer to invade the privacy, academic or otherwise, of another or the threatened invasion of the privacy of another.

4.2. Responsible use of resources

You are responsible for knowing what information resources (including networks) are available, remembering that the members of the community share them, and refraining from all acts that waste or prevent others from using these resources or from using them in whatever ways have been proscribed by the Institute and the laws of the State and Federal governments. Details regarding available resources are available in many ways, including consulting your Computing Support Representative (CSR) (see section 6.4), conferring with other users, examining on-line and printed references maintained by OIT and others, visiting the OIT Information Center, and contacting the OIT Helpdesk.

4.3. Game playing

Limited recreational game playing, that is not part of an authorized and assigned research or instructional activity, is tolerated (within the parameters of each department's rules). Institute computing and network services are not to be used for extensive or competitive recreational game playing. Recreational game players occupying a seat in a public computing facility must give up that seat when others who need to use the facility for academic or research purposes are waiting.

4.4. Information integrity

It is your responsibility to be aware of the potential for and possible effects of manipulating information, especially in electronic form, to understand the changeable nature of electronically stored information, and to verify the integrity and completeness of information that you compile or use. Do not depend on information or communications to be correct when they appear contrary to your expectations; verify it with the person who you believe originated the message or data.

4.5. Use of desktop systems

You are responsible in coordination with your CSR for the security and integrity of Institute information stored on your personal desktop system. This responsibility includes making regular disk backups, controlling physical and network access to the machine, and installing and using virus protection software. Avoid storing passwords or other information that can be used to gain access to other campus computing resources.

4.6. Access to facilities and information

4.6.1. Sharing of access

Computer accounts, passwords, and other types of authorization are assigned to individual users and must not be shared with others. You are responsible for any use of your account.

4.6.2. Permitting unauthorized access

You may not run or otherwise configure software or hardware to intentionally allow access by unauthorized users. (See section 2.2.)

4.6.3. Use of privileged access

Special access to information or other special computing privileges are to be used in performance of official duties only. Information that you obtain through special privileges is to be treated as private.

4.6.4. Termination of access

When you cease being a member of the campus community (graduate or terminate employment), or if you are assigned a new position and/or responsibilities within the Institute, your access authorization must be reviewed. You must not use facilities, accounts, access codes, privileges, or information for which you are not authorized in your new circumstances.

4.7. Attempts to circumvent security

Users are prohibited from attempting to circumvent or subvert any system's security measures. This section does not prohibit use of security tools by system administration personnel.

4.7.1. Decoding access control information

You are prohibited from using any computer program or device to intercept or decode passwords or similar access control information.

4.7.2. Denial of service

Deliberate attempts to degrade the performance of a computer system or network or to deprive authorized personnel of resources or access to any Institute computer system or network are prohibited.

4.7.3. Harmful activities

The following harmful activities are prohibited: creating or propagating viruses; disrupting services; damaging files; intentional destruction of or damage to equipment, software, or data belonging to Georgia Tech or other users; and the like.

4.7.4. Unauthorized access

You may not:

damage computer systems

obtain extra resources not authorized to you

deprive another user of authorized resources

gain unauthorized access to systems

by using knowledge of:

a special password

loopholes in computer security systems

another user's password

access abilities you used during a previous position at the Institute

4.7.5. Unauthorized monitoring

You may not use computing resources for unauthorized monitoring of electronic communications.

4.8. Academic dishonesty

You should always use computing resources in accordance with the high ethical standards of the Institute community. Academic dishonesty (plagiarism, cheating) is a violation of those standards.

4.9. Use of copyrighted information and materials

You are prohibited from using, inspecting, copying, and storing copyrighted computer programs and other material, in violation of copyright.

4.10. Use of licensed software

No software may be installed, copied, or used on Institute resources except as permitted by the owner of the software. Software subject to licensing must be properly licensed and all license provisions (installation, use, copying, number of simultaneous users, term of license, etc.) must be strictly adhered to.

4.11. Political campaigning; commercial advertising

Board of Regents policy (section 914.01) states "The use of System materials, supplies, equipment, machinery, or vehicles in political campaigns is forbidden." The Georgia Tech Faculty Handbook (section 6.15.3.8(b)) states "Political campaign and commercial advertisement shall not be displayed on the campus." The use of Institute computers and networks shall conform to these policies.

4.12. Personal business

Computing facilities, services, and networks may not be used in connection with compensated outside work nor for the benefit of organizations not related to Georgia Tech, except: in connection with scholarly pursuits (such as faculty publishing activities); in accordance with the Institute Consulting Policy or the policy Access by External Entities to Institute Information Technology Resources (OIT, 11/3/93, and any subsequent revisions); or in a purely incidental way. This and any other incidental use (such as electronic communications or storing data on single-user machines) must not interfere with other users' access to resources (computer cycles, network bandwidth, disk space, printers, etc.) and must not be excessive. State law restricts the use of State facilities for personal gain or benefit.

5. GEORGIA TECH PRIVILEGES

Our society depends on institutions like Georgia Tech to educate our citizens and advance the development of knowledge. However, in order to survive, Georgia Tech must attract and responsibly manage financial and human resources. Therefore, Tech has been granted by the State, and the various other institutions with which it deals, certain privileges regarding the information necessary to accomplish its goals and to the equipment and physical assets used in its mission.

5.1. Allocation of resources

Georgia Tech may allocate resources in differential ways in order to achieve its overall mission.

5.2. Control of access to information

Georgia Tech may control access to its information and the devices on which it is stored, manipulated, and transmitted, in accordance with the laws of Georgia and the United States and the policies of the Institute and the Board of Regents.

5.3. Imposition of sanctions

Georgia Tech may impose sanctions and punishments on anyone who violates the policies of the Institute regarding computer and network usage.

5.4. System administration access

A System Administrator (i.e., the person responsible for the technical operations of a particular machine) may access others files for the maintenance of networks and computer and storage systems, such as to create backup copies of media. However, in all cases, all individuals' privileges and rights of privacy are to be preserved to the greatest extent possible.

5.5. Monitoring of usage, inspection of files

Units of Georgia Tech operating computers and networks may routinely monitor and log usage data, such as network session connection times and end-points, CPU and disk utilization for each user, security audit trails, network loading, etc. These units may review this data for evidence of violation of law or policy, and other purposes.

When necessary, these units may monitor all the activities of and inspect the files of specific users on their computers and networks. Any person who believes such monitoring or inspecting is necessary must obtain the concurrence of the unit head and the campus Legal Division. In all cases all individuals' privileges and right of privacy are to be preserved to the greatest extent possible.

5.6. Suspension of individual privileges

Units of Georgia Tech operating computers and networks may suspend computer and network privileges of an individual for reasons relating to his/her physical or emotional safety and well being, or for reasons relating to the safety and well-being of other members of the campus community, or Institute property. Access will be promptly restored when safety and well-being can be reasonably assured, unless access is to remain suspended as a result of formal disciplinary action imposed by the Office of the Vice President for Student Services (for students) or the employee's department in consultation with the Office of Human Resources (for employees).

6. GEORGIA TECH RESPONSIBILITIES

6.1. Security procedures

Georgia Tech has the responsibility to develop, implement, maintain, and enforce appropriate security procedures to ensure the integrity of individual and institutional information, however stored, and to impose appropriate penalties when privacy is purposefully abridged.

6.2. Anti-harassment procedures

Georgia Tech has the responsibility to develop, implement, maintain, and enforce appropriate procedures to discourage harassment by use of its computers or networks and to impose appropriate penalties when such harassment takes place.

6.3. Upholding of copyrights and license provisions

Georgia Tech has the responsibility to uphold all copyrights, laws governing access and use of information, and rules of organizations supplying information resources to members of the community (e.g., acceptable use policies for use of Internet).

6.4. Individual unit responsibilities

Each unit has the responsibility of:

enforcing this policy

providing for security in their areas

providing individuals equipped with Institute-owned desktop systems with resources for regular disk backups (software, hardware, media, and training) and for virus protection

If warranted by the importance and sensitivity of information stored and processed in their facility, a unit must also:

provide system administration personnel

perform and verify integrity of regular media backups

employ appropriate security-related software and procedures

guard confidentiality of private information, including user files and system access codes

control physical access to equipment

provide proper physical environment for equipment

provide safeguards against fire, flood, theft, etc.

provide proper access administration; e.g., prompt and appropriate adjustment of access permissions upon a user's termination or transfer

control and record system software and configuration changes

monitor system logs for access control violation attempts

Units are to designate a person employed by the unit as their Computing Support Representative (CSR); the Director of Client Services, Office of Information Technology is to be notified of CSR appointments. CSRs should be knowledgeable about their unit's computing environment and about central resources and services. The CSR serves:

as the first point of contact for unit personnel seeking problem resolution, information, and other assistance regarding computing and networking

to facilitate interaction between the unit and the Office of Information Technology

6.5. Public information services

Units and individuals may, with the permission of the appropriate unit head, configure computing systems to provide information retrieval services to the public at large. (Current examples include "anonymous ftp" and "gopher.") However, in so doing, particular attention must be paid to the following sections of this policy: 2.1 (authorized use [must be consistent with Institute mission]), 3.3 (ownership of intellectual works), 4.2 (responsible use of resources), 4.9 (use of copyrighted information and materials), 4.10 (use of licensed software), and 6.4 (individual unit responsibilities). Usage of public services must not cause computer or network loading that impairs other services.

7. PROCEDURES AND SANCTIONS
7.1. Investigative contact

If you are contacted by a representative from an external organization (District Attorney's Office, FBI, GBI, Southern Bell Security Services, etc.) who is conducting an investigation of an alleged violation involving Georgia Tech computing and networking resources, inform the office of the Executive Director for Information Technology (EDIT) and the Chief Legal Advisor immediately. Refer the requesting agency to the EDIT office; that office will provide guidance regarding the appropriate actions to be taken.

7.2. Responding to security and abuse incidents

All users and units have the responsibility to report any discovered unauthorized access attempts or other improper usage of Georgia Tech computers, networks, or other information processing equipment. If you observe, or have reported to you (other than as in 7.1 above), a security or abuse problem with any Institute computer or network facilities, including violations of this policy:

Take immediate steps as necessary to ensure the safety and well-being of information resources. For example, if warranted, a system administrator should be contacted to temporarily disable any offending or apparently compromised computer accounts, or to temporarily disconnect or block offending computers from the network (see section 5.6).

Ensure that the following people are notified: (1) your Computing Support Representative, (2) your unit head, (3) the Information Resources Security Coordinator (IRSC), who is located within the Office of Information Technology.

The IRSC will coordinate the technical and administrative response to such incidents. Reports of all incidents will be forwarded to Student Services (for apparent policy violations by students) or the unit head (for employees), and to the Executive Director for Information Technology and the Chief Information Officer.

7.3. First and minor incident

If a person appears to have violated this policy, and (1) the violation is deemed minor by OIT, and (2) the person has not been implicated in prior incidents, then the incident may be dealt with at the OIT or unit level. The alleged offender will be furnished a copy of the Institute Computer and Network Usage Policy (this document), and will sign a form agreeing to conform to the policy.

7.4. Subsequent and/or major violations

Reports of subsequent or major violations will be forwarded to Student Services (for students) or the unit head (for employees) for the determination of sanctions to be imposed. Units should consult the Office of Human Resources regarding appropriate action.

7.5. Range of disciplinary sanctions

Persons in violation of this policy are subject to the full range of sanctions, including the loss of computer or network access privileges, disciplinary action, dismissal from the Institute, and legal action. Some violations may constitute criminal offenses, as outlined in the Georgia Computer Systems Protection Act and other local, state, and federal laws; the Institute will carry out its responsibility to report such violations to the appropriate authorities.

7.6. Appeals

Appeals should be directed through the already-existing procedures established for employees and students.

Chapter 8
Contingency Planning

Objective

The purpose of computer security is to protect the information services of the organization as a whole. Information should not be lost, damaged, or modified. It should be readily available to authorized users. It should not be possible to accidentally or intentionally disable the computer system.

Contingency planning is a strategy to minimize the effect of disturbances and to allow for timely resumption of activities. The aim of contingency planning is to minimize the effects of a disruption on your organization's operations. A disruption is any security violation, man-made or natural, intentional or accidental, that affects normal operations. Disruptions in computer processing can be classified into three categories:

- *Malfunctions:* Minor disruptions that affect hardware, software, or data files. They're usually quite narrow in scope, and it's usually possible to recover from them quickly.

- *Disasters:* Disruptions to the entire facility. They typically require the use of alternate off-site processing facilities to recover operations. Entire facilities may be disrupted for a significant period of time.

- *Catastrophes:* The most serious type of disruption. In a catastrophe, the facilities may have been destroyed. Alternate facilities are always needed to process data. It may be necessary to rebuild or establish new or permanent facilities.

Rarely will a company face either a disaster or a catastrophe. Malfunctions or other minor failures are likely to be the norm. For minor malfunctions, it's generally more convenient to use onsite backup facilities.

Your contingency plan should focus on the continuity of your business. Its primary purpose is to reduce the risk of financial loss and enhance your organization's ability to recover from a disruption promptly, at least cost. It should apply to all facets of your organization: staff, computer programs, data, workspace, production, and vital records. Contingency planning for your information systems should look at all critical areas including LANs and WANs, client server systems, distributed databases, and PCs.

A common mistake in contingency planning is an excessive focus on *computer* recovery. You really need a *business* recovery plan. Undue emphasis on the technology, rather than the business, is counter-productive. Quick recovery of computer technology is useless if your organization cannot recover its business. Excessive focus on computer technology results in committing too many resources to redundant processing facilities.

A contingency is an event that may or may not occur. The focus of computer security contingency planning is to provide options in case disruption strikes. Recovery from loss of key personnel is usually accomplished through succession planning and backup training. Computer facilities are typically covered by insurance policies and businesses can generally recover their investment in computers and equipment.

But losses in a disaster or catastrophe typically exceed what's recoverable through insurance policies. Some types of losses are uninsurable.

The primary focus of computer security should always be preventive rather than corrective action, though it's impossible to prevent *every* security breach. It's virtually impossible to anticipate every problem; even if a problem can be anticipated, the cost/benefit ratio may not justify taking preventive measures. Sometimes precautionary measures may prove ineffective cause of human or other error. Productivity and efficiency may also be sacrificed if precautionary measures are taken too far.

You'll need emergency procedures for each type of potential disaster. Think about how the disaster might affect data processing and business operations. How long would the service be interrupted? At what level would the company be able to operate?

Organizations are sometimes hesitant about using resources to develop a disaster or catastrophe recovery plan. The probability of a disaster or catastrophe is generally low, and the high costs associated with developing a detailed contingency plan may be a deterrent. Many organizations may feel that the costs exceed the potential benefits.

Yet while the probability of a disaster or catastrophe may be low, the cost of being unprepared is high. Most businesses are heavily dependent on computer technology; even a minor interruption could have serious financial consequences.

Contingency planning should provide an organized way to make decisions if there's a disruption. Its purpose is to reduce confusion and enhance the ability of the staff to deal with the crisis. When a disruption occurs, a company doesn't have the time to deliberate, plan, and organize its recovery. The organization needs to recover quickly. A well-tested, comprehensive recovery plan can save critical time (and therefore money).

The Role of Senior Management

Senior management has ultimate responsibility for establishing, regulating, and monitoring contingency plans. Senior management support is essential. Management must be willing to commit adequate resources, both tangible and intangible. The people at the top should appoint a team to manage the contingency planning process.

Top management has a fiduciary responsibility to protect the organization's assets. If after a disruption there are losses that could have been prevented or minimized by planning, shareholders and creditors may hold senior managers as well as the board of directors personally liable.

Government regulation, such as the Foreign Corrupt Practices Act of 1977 (FCPA), may impose additional civil and criminal penalties. The FCPA requires all publicly held organizations to maintain adequate controls over their information systems. Organizations may take reasonable steps to ensure the integrity of their records and the internal control structure. An organization that fails to protect its information records can be held in violation of the FCPA; penalties range from fines to imprisonment.

The Contingency Planning Committee

A committee should formulate, test, and implement your contingency plans; the information systems manager should be a key member, along with members from functional areas throughout the organization. The committee defines the scope of the plan, which should deal with how to:

- Prevent disruptions
- Minimize loss if a disruption cannot be prevented
- Recover from a disruption in an organized and expedient manner

The planning committee should consult with all major departments and specialists within and outside the organization before drafting a plan. Then each department should review the draft to suggest improvements and modifications. There's plenty of expertise to call on:

- *Internal auditors* will play a key role in evaluating the internal control structure and conducting operational audits. They are also familiar with the needs of external auditors.

- *The lawyers* should be consulted with respect to the legal consequences of a disruption, including compliance with government regulations, such as the FCPA.

- *The accounting and finance departments*, which are heavily dependent on information technology, are likely to suffer considerably from a disruption.

- *The security department* is responsible for coordinating the recovery efforts if there is a security breach, fire, earthquake, flood, or bomb threat.

- *Medical specialists* should be consulted for ways to protect human life in a disaster. They should know the effects of fire extinguishers, such as Halon or carbon dioxide, and other chemicals. They can advise on the type of first aid equipment that should be kept available and how employees should be trained.

- *The public relations department* should be responsible for all communications to the press and others outside the organization.

Areas to Cover

Human Safety

The primary concern in any type of planning should be the health and safety of the people who work for and with you. You need a plan for:

- Emergency evaluation

- Alerting the fire department and other emergency response authorities

- Health and safety concerns unique to the business (such as in a chemical manufacturing plant)

Business Impact Analysis

In formulating your disaster recovery plan, conduct a business impact analysis, determining the likely cost of each risk taken to a worst-case scenario. A business impact analysis considers how various threats and vulnerabilities might affect the continuity of your business. Incorporate into your plan recovery strategies for specific disasters, emphasizing your backup strategy, including the role of any off-site facilities that will be needed. Appendix 8.A contains an Impact Analysis Worksheet to help you with this.

Legal Liability

The planning committee may not realize the existence of certain liabilities during its risk analysis. The plan itself may violate certain legal requirements, exposing the organization to unnecessary liabilities.

To avoid that, the committee will need to review corporate documents, including the Articles of Incorporation and the by-laws, and then consider the impact of federal, state, and local laws on your contingency planning. Violation of laws may prevent recovery from insurance policies.

For example, the Worker Adjustment and Retraining Notification Act limits the right of an employer to lay off personnel or close a plant. Employers must provide at least 60 days notification to state and local officials as well as to employees. While natural disasters such as earthquakes are excluded from the notification requirement, other disasters—such as fires—are not. Without adequate insurance coverage, your organization may be unable to lay off personnel and must continue paying salaries and benefits to the remainder.

Flexibility

The recovery plan has to be flexible enough to cover a wide variety of disasters and catastrophes. When planning for resources, consider the effects on your business of a single disaster, such as a fire, versus the effects of a community-wide disaster, such as an earthquake or flood. In a community-wide disaster, outside resources to help your organization may be severely strained. In your contingency planning, identify the resources you will need in both types of disaster.

Notification Procedure

The notification procedure in a disaster should be clearly specified. Ask yourself:

- Who should be notified?
- How are they to be notified? What if phone lines and e-mail aren't working?
- What mobile communications equipment might be needed to provide notification?
- Who will be responsible for notification?
- Where will the primary notification list be kept? Where will the backup list be kept?
- How often should the notification list be updated?

A Communications Assessment Questionnaire is presented in Appendix 8.B.

Access to Facilities

The recovery plan has to consider the effect of delayed access to facilities after a disaster. For example, even if a fire has been put out, the authorities may not allow anyone inside the building till they've assessed the amount of structural damage. Law enforcement authorities may be conducting a criminal investigation (e.g., arson), so the building may be considered a crime scene. In a manufacturing plant there may be danger of toxic chemical contamination. In a community-wide disaster like a tornado or a flood you may not be allowed into the geographical area where your facility is located for anywhere from a couple of hours to several weeks.

Identify early those areas of the facility that require priority access. This will expedite damage assessment. If urgent access to certain areas will be required, check with local authorities before anything happens to ascertain the proper procedure. Under special circumstances, they may grant access to qualified individuals.

Emergency Acquisitions

If something goes wrong, what supplies will you need? The contingency plan should include the procedure for acquisitions during an emergency, with a list of pre-authorized emergency supplies. Specify by job title who will be responsible for emergency acquisitions, with dollar limits, and procedures to authorize expenditures beyond the limits. Any special accounting requirements should be discussed with the accounting department and incorporated into the contingency plan.

Vital Records

Vital records need to be recovered quickly from off-site backup locations. The contingency plan should specify:

- Documents and records likely to be needed first
- Where vital records are stored
- Equipment and other resources that might be needed for recovery
- Where the records will be stored once recovered

Backup Requirements

It's essential to have a backup strategy for hardware, software, data, and documentation. Backup strategy should incorporate functions that are critical for the survival of your organization. For example, data files must be backed up regularly and often. All vital records, whether or not computerized, should be protected.

Specify short-term as well as long-term needs. Contingency planning goes beyond simply keeping a backup of records for short-term recovery. In fact, it should be more focused on the long term. In the past, when computer centers tended to be centralized, traditional contingency plans focused on their recovery. With the shift to decentralized information systems, however, contingency planning must now focus on the entire organization, not simply the information processing centers or data centers.

A written backup policy will clarify procedures and prevent operational errors. The policy should specify the backup schedule for each type of data file and how long each generation of data files must be kept.

Recovery in a disaster can be expedited if your organization does not use unique hardware or software. Standard technology and up-to-date equipment and software makes replacement simple.

Backup Facilities

You need both on-site and off-site backup of hardware, software, data, and documentation. On-site backup is convenient and readily accessible; a simple fire-resistant safe may be sufficient. Store in it the most current copy of the backup files.

However, in a disaster, on-site backup tends to be inadequate. Whatever disaster—fire, earthquake, flood—affects the primary hardware, software, or data files will also affect the backup. That's why off-site backup storage is necessary.

An off-site facility may be nearby of convenience or far away for enhanced protection. A nearby facility may not be affected by a fire but may be susceptible to damage from natural disasters like earthquakes or hurricanes. For a local off-site facility a fire-resistant safe in a building within a mile or two may provide adequate protection.

A remote off-site facility provides still greater protection. A fire-resistant storage area several miles away may be accessed weekly and used to house data files for at least several weeks. A very remote off-site facility—preferably at least 100 miles away—provides the greatest protection and may be used for archival storage.

Larger organizations will typically keep several generations of backups in different facilities. The logistics of moving files to different facilities can become complex; you'll need procedures to ensure that data files are correctly backed up and transported to the right facilities.

Backup sites may be categorized into three types:

- *Hot sites:* Sites that can become fully operational on short notice, typically a few hours. All hardware and software must be compatible with the original site.

- *Warm sites:* Sites that can become fully operational in a matter of days or weeks. Less expensive equipment and software may already be in place. More expensive equipment or software is purchased or leased if there is a serious disruption. A partial degradation in processing output is considered acceptable.

- *Cold sites:* Sites that have only a skeleton structure in place. It may take anywhere from several days to weeks or even months to get the site operational. Hardware and software are not in place, but there is adequate electrical wiring and air conditioning.

While hot sites offer considerably faster recovery time, their cost is high. Warm sites are less expensive; cold sites are typically useful for longer-term computing needs. An organization may wish to use all three types of sites in its recovery plan. For example, a hot site could be established for short-term processing needs, giving the company enough time to prepare a warm or cold site for the long run.

For critical applications where a delay in computer processing may cause significant financial loss, you can subscribe to a commercial hot site. Though the cost is high, these sites will guarantee that you'll have properly configured hardware and software to run your data when you really need it.

The costs of commercial hot sites vary considerably. Most vendors charge a monthly subscription fee plus an activation fee and an hourly rate when you actually need to use the site. The activation fee and the hourly rates may be covered by insurance.

Some vendors charge a very high activation fee to discourage use in non-emergency situations. Others encourage their subscribers to use the facilities for non-emergency situations such as overload processing.

Commercial hot sites should not be relied on for an extended period of time. For longer-term needs, there are also commercial warm and cold sites. A warm site subscription typically provides for basic computer facilities with some hardware. The cold site typically provides the infrastructure for a computer facility, such as air conditioning, heating, and humidity controls; wiring for voice and data; electrical wiring; and flood and fire protection. It usually does not contain hardware or software.

In choosing a commercial hot site, consider the number and concentration of subscribers. Too many means that the facility may not be available when needed; too few raises concerns about the financial survival of the business. Look out for a geographic concentration of subscribers: If there's a natural disaster, the site may be unable to meet the needs of all its subscribers.

When you're selecting a hot site, take into account:

- Activation fees
- Monthly fees
- Usage fees
- Contract period and penalty for early termination
- Number of subscribers
- Geographical concentration of subscribers
- Networking capacity
- Customer service and technical assistance

- Hardware and software provided
- Ability to upgrade hardware and software if necessary
- Vendor's expertise and experience in your industry
- Vendor's financial stability
- Vendor's experience with actual disasters
- References
- Other services provided

Mobile backup sites are available from several vendors. These are trailers equipped with computer hardware and software that can be taken to any location you desire. This setup is especially helpful where it may be difficult for the personnel to commute to a remote backup facility.

To identify the best recovery strategy you'll need to conduct a thorough technical as well as cost-benefit analysis. Don't forget how much it costs for wiring, air conditioning, and fire prevention.

Mutual Aid Agreements

Mutual aid agreements are a low-cost alternative for emergency processing: Two or more organizations with similar equipment and applications promise to help each other in an emergency. These agreements may not be legally enforceable so they shouldn't be relied on exclusively, but they make sense especially for companies with special requirements that may be unable to use commercial hot sites.

If you're thinking about a mutual aid agreement, ask yourself:

- What are the differences in equipment between my company and the potential partner?
- What are the differences in applications?
- How will we maintain compatibility in equipment and software with the partner over time?
- How often will we test our systems for compatibility?
- In an emergency, how much processing time will they have available? If there are multiple partners, which one will we use?
- What equipment, software, staff assistance, and facilities will the partner provide?

- How long will it take before we can use the partner's facilities?
- How long can we use the partner's facilities?

Relocating Facilities

The severity of the damage to your own facilities will dictate whether your organization relocates temporarily or permanently. The contingency plan should cover both possibilities. Recovering from a disaster may take a long time; what happens in the interim? For example, if only a portion of your facilities can be used:

- Which departments or functions will go back in first?
- What type of support will they require?
- Can large departments be split up, operating out of two or more locations?

Factors to think about with regard to relocating include:

- Square footage needed
- Which departments need to be in proximity
- Communications facilities needed
- Security concerns
- Storage area needed
- Access to public transportation
- Parking needed
- Employee requirements, such as housing, schools, day care, etc. (if relocating at a distance)

Hardware Backup

Many organizations think that hardware backup is all that's needed for contingency planning, but hardware backup alone is not sufficient for most companies. While hardware is an essential element of contingency planning, there's a lot more to it.

It *is* important to have backup hardware available both on and off-site. For smaller disruptions, only one or at most a few pieces of equipment are likely to be affected. On-site backup is usually sufficient to resolve such problems. To save on costs you might consider using older or slower systems in emergencies. Sometimes partial processing capability is acceptable.

For more serious disruptions, which tend to be longer, off-site hardware is of considerable importance. While hardware vendors are naturally the best source for replacement equipment, the vendor may be unable to supply the equipment you need quickly enough for you. If that's so, used hardware dealers may be able to supply critical components on short notice.

Software and Data Backup

Software and data are intangible assets that must be protected. Software includes the operating system, utilities, and application programs. Keep backup copies not only of your primary software but also of any upgrades or patches to fix bugs, and of user manuals (online or hard copy). It's unnecessary to keep backup copies of older generation software.

You need backup copies of the software and user manuals at both primary and off-site facilities, where you also need copies of the software configuration files or other special settings. Don't forget to upgrade software at both facilities at the same time, and set in place a procedure to ensure that copies of maintenance patches to the software are also kept off-site. Check the legal requirements for making backups: Some vendors require an additional licensing fee if the software will be used in an alternate facility.

Data includes all source documents, electronic data files and databases, and output documents. Unlike software, data by its very nature changes continuously. The contingency plan should prepare for rapid recovery of data.

There are several different techniques for backing up data. For small files the process may be as simple as making a duplicate on the backup medium. When it's either not practical or not cost-effective to backup the entire file, try something else.

In a batch processing system, a new master file is created using the old master and updating it with transactional changes. Keeping copies of the old master file for two or three generations, along with copies of the transaction file updates, provides for continuous backup of the data.

A real-time online processing system requires different procedures. Duplicate logging of transactions may be necessary. Copies of individual records may have to be kept before updating. Other techniques, such as before-and-after images of master records, may be useful. Specialized backup procedures are typically an integral part of database management systems.

Before recovering data from backup files, it's advisable always to duplicate the backup files to prevent accidents. Data integrity during the reconstruction process can then be ensured with special supervision and controls.

Documentation Backup

Along with hardware, software, and data, backup user manuals and other documentation should be stored in an off-site fire-resistant location. When changes are made to the primary manuals and documentation, make sure that the backup documentation is updated as well.

Systems and program documentation that should be backed up include:

- Source code for programs
- Flowcharts
- Program logic descriptions
- Error conditions

Vital Records and Source Documents

While most organizations store backup copies of vital records off-site, there are still numerous documents that may only be in the primary facilities because they have not yet been backup up. Many of these are source documents like invoices or purchase orders that originate outside the organization. If a source document is critical and the information in it cannot be easily reconstructed if the document is destroyed, you need a procedure to copy the source document.

Remote Backup

Several companies offer remote backup using the Internet. Periodically, usually once a day, your data files can be automatically backed up to an off-site computer facility where the data is stored encrypted. Companies that offer remote backup include:

- At Backup, Inc.: *http://www.atbackup.com/*
- Atrieva: *http://www.atrieva.com/*
- BACKUP Data Protection Agency: *http://members.aol.com/backupdpa/index.htm*
- Connected Corporation: *http://www.connected.com/*

- CYBeRGEM Remote Backup System: *http://www.cybrgem.com/backup/*
- DataLock Remote Data Services: *http://datalock.com/*
- Filetron: *http://www.back-up.com/*
- Guardian Computer Service: *http://www.guardiancomputer.com/*
- Netsafe: *http://www.evault.com/*
- Offsite Data Management Remote Backup Service: *http://odms.com/*
- Saf-T-Net: *http://www.trgcomm.com/*
- SafeGuard Interactive: *http://www.sgii.com/*
- TeleBackup Systems, Inc.: *http://www.telebackup.com/*

A more costly alternative is to transmit a copy of each transaction to a remote facility. In *mirror processing* the data is not only transmitted but also updated on a duplicate database. With mirror processing the backup database is always current. This doesn't necessarily have to be done at a remote location; you may want to set it up on-site.

Fire Safety

Fire is the most common cause of damage to computer centers. Combustible material should not be allowed in any computer room. Install fire-detectors in vulnerable locations. Use fire-retardant material for office furniture, draperies, and any floor coverings. Put waste receptacles outside the computer room: Computer paper in waste receptacles can accelerate a fire.

Detection Devices

Fire detectors sense either thermal combustion and its byproducts or changes in temperature. They may be actuated by smoke, heat, or flame. All detectors must meet government standards. Make sure the devices are connected to an automatic fire alarm system.

Smoke-actuated devices provide early warning of fires developing slowly. They should be installed in all air conditioning and ventilating systems. Smoke detectors typically rely on either *photoelectric* or *radioactive* devices.

In the photoelectric cell, variations in the intensity of light cause changes in electric current. These detectors are generally of three types:

- *Area-sampling* devices draw in air from the area to be protected: If smoke is present in the sampled air, the light reflections on the photoelectric cell will trigger the alarm.

- *Beam* devices focus a beam of light onto a photoelectric cell from across the protected area. Smoke causing an obstruction in the light activates the alarm.

- *Spot* devices, unlike beam devices, contain the light source and the receiver in one unit. Smoke entering the detector causes the light to reflect onto the photoelectric cell, activating the alarm.

Radioactive smoke detectors contain a minute amount of radioactive material in a special housing (the danger from radiation from such devices is minimal). Smoke interacting with the radioactive material changes its ionization, which activates the alarm. Radioactive detectors are mostly commonly *spot* types.

The response time for radioactive smoke detectors is affected by several variables, including the stratification of air currents and the nature of the combustion products. Generally, the heavier the particles resulting from combustion, the longer it takes for them to reach the ceiling, where the smoke detectors are usually attached, and the longer the response time of the unit.

Heat-actuated detectors can be of two types. The first will activate the alarm when the temperature reaches a predetermined value. The second senses the amount of change in temperature. Typically, when the rise in temperature exceeds 15° to 20° F. the alarm is activated.

In highly combustible areas, the rate-of-rise temperature detectors are recommended because their response time is faster. However, fixed temperature detectors are not as prone to false alarms. Some heat-actuated detectors contain both types of sensors.

Heat detectors are available in line or spot styles. *Line-type* detectors usually rely on heat-sensitive cables or a pneumatic tube. *Spot-type* detectors are placed at fixed intervals in each zone.

Flame-actuated detectors are of two types, both expensive: flame-radiation-frequency and flame-energy. *Flame-radiation-frequency* detectors sense the flame-related flicker caused by combustion. Flame-energy detectors sense the infrared energy of the flame. They tend to be best-suited to protecting expensive equipment; their principal advantage is that they are super-fast. These detectors can also produce enough voltage to trigger the release of an extinguishing agent.

Extinguishing Agents

Different types of fires require different types of extinguishing agents. Using the wrong extinguishing agent can do more harm than good.

- Fires fed by *ordinary combustible materials*, such as wood, paper, plastics, and fabric, can be safety extinguished with water or tri-class (ABC) dry chemical.

- Fires fed by *flammable liquids and gases*, such as oil, grease, gasoline, or paint, can generally be safely extinguished with tri-class (ABC) dry chemical, halon, FM-200, and carbon dioxide.

- Fires involving *live electrical equipment* should be extinguished only with a non-conducting agent such as tri-class (ABC), regular dry chemical, halon, or carbon dioxide.

Hand-held fire extinguishers should be mounted on the wall, as should self-contained breathing apparatus, because carbon dioxide discharge can suffocate humans.

Electrical Fires

Most computer room fires will be electrical, caused by overheating of wire insulation or other components. Because smoke from an electrical fire may be toxic, it should be avoided even in small quantities. Generally electrical fires cannot be extinguished until the heat source is eliminated.

A power panel with circuit breakers for the major pieces of equipment should be easily accessible, preferably inside the computer room. The circuits should be clearly labeled so that equipment can be shut down quickly in an emergency. There should be separate circuits for redundant devices, and an emergency switch to shut down everything if there is a fire.

In a major fire or explosion, the only concern should be the safety of human life. Computer equipment and wiring is likely to be destroyed by the intense heat. That's why backup copies of disks and data should always be kept off-site. Not only will this help in recovering from a fire, it can also help during the fire since the staff will not be tempted to risk their lives saving data.

Carbon dioxide, a colorless, odorless, and electrically non-conductive inert gas, is generally stored under pressure as a liquid. Carbon dioxide extinguishes fire by reducing the amount of oxygen available to it. It may not be effective on fires fed by materials such as metal hydrides, reactive metals like sodium, potassium, magnesium, titanium, and zirconium, and chemicals containing oxygen available for combustion (for more information, see *http://www.afaefire.co.uk/htlm/carbon_dioxide.html*).

Halon has the potential of depleting the ozone layer. While halon is still in use, by international agreement it has not been manufactured since January 1, 1994. FM-200, a substitute, is not very effective against electrical fires. In an electrical fire, it's essential that the power be shut off because till power is stopped a fire extinguishing system will only suppress, not extinguish, the fire.

The suppression agent in FM-200 is a halogenated alkane, heptafluoropropane. Under compression FM-200, a colorless and odorless gas, becomes a liquid, which is stored in steel cylinders.

Once discharged, FM-200 returns to the gaseous state. It suppresses fire by cooling it and reducing the amount of oxygen available. It's typically discharged rapidly, in no more than a few seconds. FM-200 helps prevent re-ignition. It doesn't leave any residue, it doesn't require cleanup after discharge, and it doesn't harm humans.

Water Sprinklers

Water sprinkler systems are a simple, relatively inexpensive protection against fire. Most new buildings are required by code to have sprinkler systems, though their accidental activation can cause substantial damage and it may take a long time before normal operations can be resumed.

In an electrical fire, water may even intensify the fire, causing greater damage. Sensors should therefore be installed to cut off electrical power before sprinklers are turned on. It should also be possible to activate sprinkler heads individually to prevent damage to a wide area. A shut-off valve inside the computer room can help you shut off water when it's no longer needed, minimizing damage if the system is accidentally activated.

Carbon dioxide, halon, and FM-200 extinguishers don't require any cleanup after discharge. Foam or dry chemicals can be hard to remove. Quick removal of smoke should be a priority. The smoke or fire alarm should automatically activate special fans and blowers.

Extinguishing Micro-computer Fires

If computer equipment starts smoking, first cut off the equipment's electrical power. This is often sufficient to extinguish the fire by itself. If there are visible signs of fire, or if you can feel the heat, use a fire extinguisher.

Carbon dioxide extinguishers are often recommended for microcomput-
er-related fires. When using a carbon dioxide extinguisher, don't spray
the agent directly onto the surface of the CRT because the sudden drop in
temperature it causes will shatter the glass.

Training

Personnel should be trained for a fire emergency. Company policy should
state exactly what action should be taken if a fire starts or a smoke alarm
goes off. Personnel should be strictly prohibited from risking injury or
loss of life to protect data or equipment.

Preventing Damage

The following steps can reduce the damage caused by fire, and in the
process reduce your insurance premiums:

- Safes for storage of documents should have a minimum four-hour
  fire rating.
- Walls, floors, and ceilings of computer facilities should have a
  minimum two-hour fire rating.
- The fire alarm should ring simultaneously at the computer facility
  and the nearest fire station. In addition, fire alarm signals should
  be located to assure prompt response.
- Vaults storing backup tapes and records should be in a separate
  building at a sufficient distance.
- Smoke and ionization detection systems should be installed on the
  ceiling of the computer facilities. Water detection systems should
  be installed under the floors.
- Halon, FM-22, or a similar chemical extinguishing system should
  be installed throughout the facilities. Automatic sprinkler systems
  can be used in supply and support areas.
- Building code and fire marshal regulations must be adhered to
  strictly.

FireTracer and WinTracer

FireTracer products (http://www.emss.net) give the exact location of the
source of a developing fire in a computer cabinet, control equipment set,
or room. They can also be used for air handling units, return air grills,
ducts, and large open areas, supported by air sampling techniques. With

these products, air is pumped into a series of micro-bore tubes positioned in a cabinet, room, or compartment being protected. The sample of air is then analyzed for the presence of either smoke particles or gas. If the smoke level reaches a preset trace level, then the FireTracer switches from a sampling mode to a search mode to identify the exact location of the smoke source.

Three separate alarms are triggered by the system. The first alarm level is triggered when the trace cycle is initiated. A pre-alarm is triggered to warn that a potential fire exists in the identified area. The final alarm indicates that a full incipient fire condition is present. Each of the three alarms may be connected to a fire panel for control purposes.

WinTracer control software may be used to monitor and control FireTracers. WinTracer provides:

- Warning when smoke levels exceed preset limits
- Location of the alarm
- Action sequences and hazard indications
- Remote control [reset, off/online & changing functions, such as alarm levels, etc.]
- Display of site status [tracers which are on/offline, etc.]
- Historical trends
- Data logging and recording of significant events

The basic display is simple enough to be monitored by an unskilled operator. Bar graphs display current levels of smoke or gas. Color-coding indicates when current levels exceed the alert levels. If there is an alarm, there is a text description of the alarm source, supplemented by a site map pinpointing the location, along with actions to be taken for different alarm types and locations (e.g., notes to tell operator to phone fire station, clear room, whatever) and a list of hazards near the alarm locations.

WinTracer can be customized and the data analyzed. The administrator has remote programming access to change text descriptions, action sequences, and hazard lists. Alarms may be acknowledged or cancelled. Trend graphs can be plotted to monitor compliance.

Insurance

Your insurance, with the right endorsements, must be adequate to protect against disruptions in business. Your contingency plan should address insurance concerns both before and after a disaster. Especially be sure you're covered if access to the facilities is delayed.

Standard insurance policies treat computer equipment like industrial equipment, covering them for the same threats. Standard policies don't cover computer equipment for power outages or electrostatic discharges that may delete or destroy electronically stored information.

A policy specifically geared toward electronic data processing (EDP) typically covers risks to computers, including replacement or repair. For all high-technology assets, the policy should contain a *replacement cost* endorsement. Unlike assets like industrial machinery with a long life and low depreciation, computer equipment tends to depreciate rapidly, losing its value. Without the replacement cost endorsement, you may not be able to afford to replace computer equipment after a disaster.

EDP policies, however, typically don't cover damages resulting from loss or inability to access computer equipment. That's why you need business interruption and out-of-pocket expenses insurance. *Business interruption* insurance covers not only losses caused directly by the disaster, but also future business losses if operations can't resume quickly. *Out-of-pocket expense* coverage reimburses you for use of alternate computer facilities. Make sure your operations at the outsourcing vendor's facilities are covered.

Keep your insurance policies up to date. Many organizations just keep on renewing a policy they bought years ago, though the business environment is continuously changing. A policy that provided adequate coverage even three years ago may fall short for current needs.

Maintain a running list of organizational assets, along with their appraised values, updating it every time an asset is added or retired. Certainly review it at least once or twice a year. And, of course, store a copy of the list off-site.

Many insurance policies require policyholders to insure their property to 80%, 90%, or 100% of its value, penalizing them if they fail to maintain the proper level. To reduce your chances of being penalized, have your assets appraised periodically and insured to the value required by the policy.

Check that your *valuable papers and records* coverage includes the cost of recreating documents, such as re-entering data and restoring damaged items.

Software products are often excluded from insurance policies unless there is a specific endorsement, but you need to have them covered in case there's a breakdown in equipment, such as a system crash.

Appendix 8.C discusses how to implement an effective insurance recovery program. Appendix 8.D discusses how to save time and money if you need to file an insurance claim.

Conclusion

Many organizations have no workable disaster recovery plan. A common mistake is to put too much emphasis on electronic data processing and computer recovery and too little on keeping the business running. Many business functions may be able to survive with manual procedures; prepare procedures to support the essential functions of your business until computer processing is re-established.

Both user participation and the support of senior management are critical in formulating an effective contingency plan.

Many contingency plans provide unnecessary details and lack flexibility. Too much information makes it difficult to update and revise the plan. Anything that can be dealt with at the time of the disaster should be left out, as should anything that cannot be determined until the effect of a disaster has been evaluated.

Contingency plans should be reviewed, tested, and updated at least annually. At each review ask yourself:

- What does the organization need now and in the future to survive after a disaster?

- How are these needs likely to be fulfilled by the strategies selected in the plan?

- How can the strategies be made more effective?

Those who were responsible for developing the contingency plan should not review, test, or evaluate it. Independent individuals will have greater objectivity and insight.

Disasters or catastrophes are extremely rare. It's therefore imperative that your contingency plan be cost-effective, though the cost-benefit analysis is admittedly very difficult for rare events. Furthermore, your company's risk preference will affect how much risk you can tolerate.

Senior managers are ultimately responsible for contingency planning. While they may delegate many details to middle management and staff, they must play an integral part in the creation of the plan.

Appendix 8.A: Business Impact Analysis Worksheet[1]

What would be the effect of a worst-case scenario if any kind of disaster or calamity occurred at your work facility? Calculating the "impact value" of a crisis will tell you how damaging a critical incident will be if there is no crisis intervention.

Amount of Scrutiny the Crisis Might Generate
- What kind of news coverage might ensure?
- What kind of agencies might get involved? OSHA? EPA?
- How would stockholders react?
- What about senior management's reaction and handling of event?

On a scale of 1 to 10, how much scrutiny would your crisis incur?

Company's Public Image
- How will the public view the crisis and your handling of it?
- Will the company be seen as culpable? Liable?
- What about the reactions of customers?
- Community reaction?
- Reaction of employees' families?

On a scale of 1 to 10, estimate the potential damage to company image and reputation in the aftermath of the crisis.

Effect on Employee Morale and Productivity
- How would the crisis affect employee productivity?
- Absenteeism?
- How much time might be spent dealing with the crisis at the expense of other work functions?
- What about employee morale during this time? Stress? Outrage?

On a scale of 1 to 10, estimate the amount of business interference the crisis might generate as a result of its effect on employees.

---

[1]This appendix, taken from Dan Paulk, "Estimating the Impact Value of a Crisis" (available through *http:// www.disaster-resource.com/*), is based on the research of Steven Fink, *Crisis Management: Planning for the Inevitable* (New York: American Management Association, 1986).

Damage to the Company's Bottom Line

• What might be the cost in "hard" dollars to the company?

• How much would be covered by insurance?

• In terms of "soft" dollars, what will employee unrest, stress, absenteeism, lowered morale, and lowered productivity cost the company?

• How would a crisis affect the company's ability to get products to market on time? Meet payroll? Pay creditors?

• What about the costs of increased workers' compensation claims?

• Unemployment insurance claims?

Combining hard and soft-dollar costs, what is your opinion (1 to 10) of the cost of the crisis?

Legal Liability/Vulnerability

• Was this incident foreseeable?

• If so, did we take enough reasonable precautions to prevent the calamity?

• Did we have any specific controls or policies in place to prevent the crisis?

• Is there any "discoverable" information regarding this incident that could be interpreted in a damning way by outsiders?

• Would an aggressive plaintiff's attorney smell an opportunity here?

Considering the potential degree of legal liability, what is your estimate (1 to 10) of legal vulnerability regarding this incident.

Impact Value of the Crisis = Total of 5 scores divided by 5: _____

The effect of a crisis on business functions increases as the impact value score increases. The score tells you how damaging a "critical incident" will be if there is no crisis intervention.

Appendix 8.B: Communications Assessment Questionnaire[1]

1. Who is responsible for ensuring that backup communications are established?

2. What are your existing communications capabilities?
    A. Voice: _____
    B. Data: _____
    C. Image transmission: _____

3. Inventory your existing backup communications.
    A. Radio: _____
    B. Cellular: _____
    C. Amateur radio: _____
    D. Data/fax: _____
    E. Public telephones: _____
    F. Essential service: _____
    G. Other: _____

4. Who plans to use these backup communications during a disaster? (Identify specific work groups or people—chances are several people think they're going to use the same backups.)

5. What are your critical circuits? What alternate communications capability do you have for them?

6. What are your critical systems? What alternate communications or backup protection do you have for them?

7. Which systems have backup power? How long will it last? What are your plans to have backup generators available if needed?

8. What priorities have been established of communications restoration by:
    A. Location
    B. Systems/switches
    C. Facilities

9. What are your alternative routing patterns? Are they activated automatically, or can you redirect your traffic routes at the time of a disaster? What are your plans to redirect traffic, if you can?

---

[1] This appendix is taken from Judy Bell, "Communications Assessment Questionnaire" (Disaster Survival Planning, Inc., *http://www.disaster-survival.com*).

10. What emergency restoration procedures have you established with your communications and equipment vendors?

11. Where do you store your communications information? How is it preserved as a vital record?

12. Who in your organization will need backup communications at the time of a disaster?

13. Who do they primarily need to talk to?

14. What will they use as their alternate communications if they aren't at work when the disaster strikes?

15. Based on all the information examined, what do you recommend for alternate communications for each department and critical member of your organization?

Appendix 8.C: Insurance Recovery Program[1]

The following ten steps will help your organization implement an effective insurance recovery program:

1. Determine accurate corporate asset values based on either actual cash or replacement values. Cash value is the original cash value of the asset minus the time depreciation of the asset. Replacement value is what it would cost to replace the asset.

2. Estimate recovery expenses by conducting several what-if scenarios to determine how much insurance you will need to cover out-of-pocket expenses related to the recovery of the information technology and corporate assets. This would include hot site declaration, daily usage fees, overtime, and travel.

3. Determine the business income coverage amount by completing a Business Impact Analysis (BIA; see Appendix 8.A). If the BIA shows that your company would not have the cash reserves to meet forecasted operating expenses, consider business income insurance. This is expensive, so run your financial models carefully.

4. Determine the coinsurance amount by accurately assessing how much insurance you need to carry. If you don't carry insurance on a reasonable value of your assets, you will only collect a percentage of the actual loss rather than the full amount. The industry standard of coinsurance—a strategy designed to lower insurance premiums—is 80 percent, so if you have assets of $1 million, you need to be insured for at least $800,000. That's why you need an up-to-date inventory—it's very easy to fall below the coinsurance amount, especially during times of inflation.

5. Request a premium reduction review. Many insurance companies offer a discount to companies that have a formalized loss prevention program. They also have risk managers who can advise you on how to make the loss prevention program more effective. This can save you 20 percent or more on premiums, depending on the sophistication of your program.

---

[1] This appendix is based on Tari Shreider's, "Insurance: The Disaster Recovery Plan of Last Resort," *Contingency Planning and Management*, June 1996.

6. Properly insure proprietary software. Media coverage pays for the cost of replacement or reproduction only. On the other hand, commercial software is easily replaced for a nominal fee.

7. Know your policy exclusions. Many companies have made insurance claims only to find that their policy specifically excludes coverage for their most common risks. Look for the fine print regarding utility failures, media restoration, earthquakes, and other exclusions. Review exclusions for computer equipment used during travel or at employees' homes, since many policies specially exclude coverage for equipment at locations not listed on the policy. Policy exclusions can be altered with a rider.

8. See if you're over-insured in some areas. Today, when many hardware manufacturers provide recovery and restoration insurance in lease agreements, you may be doubly insured. Worse, manufacturers may be considered the primary carrier if the insurance they provide is more comprehensive than a policy written elsewhere.

9. Put the policy out for competitive bid. More than 50 major companies underwrite business recovery policies. Placing your company's insurance needs out for competitive bid could save you as much as 40 percent on your premiums.

10. Document your insurance response plan. If a disaster strikes your company, this will be one of the most vital documents you have. It specifies the roles and responsibilities of your company and the insurance company after a disaster. Just following the procedures set forth by the insurance carrier could allow them to adjust the claim, which could waive your company's rights to dispute it.

Appendix 8.D: Making an Insurance Claim[1]

If you need to make a claim to obtain reimbursement from your insurance company for damages, the following will help you save time and money.

Hire a Reputable Claims Adjuster: A specialist experienced in dealing with insurance company claims adjusters can substantially increase your settlement.

Document the Loss: Insurance companies require extensive documentation of losses before paying any claims. It's not unusual for a final settlement check to be issued years after the disaster. Proper documentation will shorten the time.

Arrange for a Special Loss-Payable Clause: Insurance policies often cover several parties under one policy. Placing and negotiating a claim under this circumstance could require 10 or more endorsements before a settlement check is issued. Get a power of attorney or a waiver from other parties.

Reduce the Risk of Additional Loss: Insurance companies will pay for physical damage to the property for the peril insured against, but if additional damage occurs after the event and your company could have avoided or reduced that loss, payment may be forfeited. Board up those windows, get a fence up, do whatever can be done to secure what's left of the property against new risks.

---

[1] This appendix is based on Tari Shreider, "Insurance: The Disaster Recovery Plan of Last Resort," *Contingency Planning and Management,* June 1996.

Chapter 9
Auditing and
Legal Issues

Introduction

Most organizations are facing a host of technologies ranging from e-commerce, the Internet, the Intranet, data mining, data analysis, data warehousing, and telecommunications to enterprise-wide applications, artificial intelligence expert systems and neural networks, and client-server computing. All business processes today depend on effective and efficient information processing.

Laws and public policies to regulate the use of these technologies have not kept pace with their development. For example, legal boundaries to protect confidentiality and integrity of data are of concern to security professionals.

Security Auditing

The field of security auditing may be broadly classified into two types, internal and external. Both rely on the independent appraisal function. However, their scope is different.

Internal auditors typically work for a given organization. External auditors do not. They are typically Certified Public Accountants (CPAs) or Chartered Accountants (CAs) hired to perform an independent audit, usually of a company's financial statements. Their primary concern is to evaluate the fairness of the statements.

The scope of internal auditing is typically broader. Internal auditors are concerned not only with safeguarding organizational assets but also with promoting operational efficiency. Their concern is that the company have adequate controls and that the procedures used are cost-efficient as well as effective. Internal auditors typically report to top management or to the audit committee of the board of directors.

The information technology (IT) function can be audited by both internal and external auditors. Whoever does it must have expertise in both financial auditing and computer technology. IT auditors can help your company assess the risks related to the use of computer technology.

Coordinating the activities of IT auditors and financial auditors can enhance audit efficiency. IT auditors might train and guide non-IT auditors in IT procedures and methods. Or IT auditors might manage the computer system during financial audit processing.

IT auditors recommend appropriate controls, which tend to be more complex than controls in manual systems. Specialized computer audit techniques must be used in highly automated environments. IT auditing:

- Uses technological tools and expertise

- Evaluates the adequacy and effectiveness of the control systems

- Assesses technology-related risks

IT auditors review systems to ensure that they meet quality criteria, assessing their compliance with the organization's systems development methodology. IT auditors may review proposed enhancements to computer systems to evaluate whether the system contains adequate controls. Their participation in the development process avoids the need to modify systems after they've been implemented, a costly and difficult process. It may in fact sometimes be virtually impossible to correctly modify a system.

While IT auditors may evaluate systems in process, the IT auditor must not assume any operational responsibility. The auditors must remain independent and objective.

Data centers serve the information needs of an organization. IT auditors typically review the following aspects of data centers:

- Systems development standards

- Efficiency and effectiveness of operating and administrative procedures

- Library control procedures

- Structure of the data center

- Network system

- Backup controls

- Contingency planning and disaster recovery
- Personnel practices
- Security

To perform their duties IT auditors must:

- Keep current with state-of-the-art technologies
- Understand how to use the technology to support business functions
- Use audit tools specific to the technology needs of the organization

IT auditors often review applications systems, with special attention to programmed control procedures such as edit checks and exception reporting. Among their duties, IT auditors:

- Evaluate the risks and controls associated with technology
- Support other auditing functions during financial, operational, or compliance audits
- Evaluate corporate computer policy and security standards

The IT auditor is also responsible for determining whether controls are adequate and whether:

- Transactions are processed accurately and completely
- Transactions are properly authorized
- Errors and omissions are prevented or detected
- Duties are segregated
- Jobs are completed in a timely fashion

IT auditors often assist external and operational internal auditors in:

- Collecting, extracting, and analyzing data
- Reviewing and testing internal controls
- Investigating exceptions

Transaction Trail

The transaction trail or audit trail allows the auditor to trace a transaction back to its origins. All attempts to gain access to the system should be logged chronologically. Unusual activity and variations from established procedures should be identified and investigated.

Many significant transactions occur inside the computer, so they aren't visible or directly observable. The transaction trail provides information about additions, deletions, or modifications to data within the system. An effective audit trail allows the data to be retrieved and certified. Audit trails will give information such as:

- Date and time of the transaction
- Who processed the transaction
- At which terminal the transaction was processed

Maintaining audit trails is more difficult in an electronic environment. In a paper-based system, for instance, a physical purchase order is prepared, typically in triplicate. At each state, paper work is done and a physical trail established. Such a trail is normally absent in electronic transactions.

Your computer software should be designed to provide an audit trail. Most commercial software packages have at least some audit trail capability.

Computer security risks affect an organization's internal control structure, which in turn affects the ability to audit the entity. Computer processing reduces human involvement, centralizes data, and may eliminate segregation of duties. Centralizing data makes it possible to introduce higher quality controls over operations. However, due to reduced human involvement and less segregation of duties, auditors must use great care in evaluating the electronic data processing department.

Adequate segregation of duties is crucial. No person should be in a position both to perpetrate and to conceal errors in the normal course of business. For example, there should be a division of duties between:

- *Programmers, librarians, and operators:* Different individuals should develop computer applications, have custody of programs and data files, and operate applications.
- *Data processing personnel, users, and control personnel*

- *Individuals authorizing changes in program logic or data and those coding the changes*

EDI and Electronic Contracting

Electronic data interchange (EDI) systems are on-line systems where computers automatically perform transactions such as order processing and generating invoices. EDI allows trading partners to exchange electronic data faster, cheaper, and more accurately. The messages are structured in a prearranged format to facilitate automatic computer processing. The electronic messages generally result in a legally binding contract.

Although EDI can reduce costs, it can adversely affect an auditor's ability to do her job. EDI transactions go through several systems. Electronic records and audit trail must be maintained throughout. Any data used for EDI needs to be translated into a standardized format; the translation software must maintain the audit trail. Any communication sent over the network must be accounted for by communication software. Data translated into internal format by the recipient's translation software must be tracked. Finally, the data is used by the recipient's application software.

In an EDI environment, a weakness in any system can create problems not just for that entity but also for its trading partners. Therefore, each function at each stage must be reviewed and appropriate controls incorporated.

The American Institute of Certified Public Accountants (AICPA) has issued control techniques to ensure the integrity of an EDI system. The AICPA recommends that controls over accuracy and completeness at the application level include:

- Checks on performance to determine compliance with industry standards
- Checks on sequence numbering for transactions
- Prompt reporting of irregularities
- Verification of adequacy of audit trails
- Checks of embedded headers and trailers at interchange, functional group, and transaction set level

Control techniques at the environmental level include:

- Quality assurance review of vendor software
- Segregation of duties
- Ensuring that software is virus-free
- Procuring an audit report from the vendor's auditors
- Evidence of testing

To ensure that all EDI transactions are authorized, the AICPA suggests these controls:

- Operator identification code
- Operator profile
- Trading partner identifier
- Maintenance of user access variables
- Regular changing of passwords

Not all electronic messages result in electronic contracting. For example, messages with purely informational content don't. Nor do intrafirm messages; the law generally distinguishes between intra-firm and inter-firm communications.

Yet electronic contracting occurs routinely. Examples of electronic offer and acceptance modes are:

- Purchase orders
- Invoices
- Payments
- Solicitation and submission of bids
- Filing documents with the government
- Advertising goods and services

Trading partner agreements or EDI agreements are essential to electronic contracting. These agreements:

- Clarify each party's rights and obligations

- Specify the risk and liability of each party
- Help avoid misunderstandings

A trading partner agreement gives the parties the legal right to enforce it. These agreements affect partners only; they don't cover third parties, such as VANs. The legal and EDI communities (e.g., the American Bar Association and the EDI Council of Canada) have drafted several model trading partner agreements. There are also model agreements for specific industries and countries. Though the models provide a fair and balanced contract, most businesses will want to customize them to their own needs.

A trading partner agreement should state the intent of the parties to transact business electronically. It should specify whether all trade or only a specified portion of the trade between the two parties is covered by the agreement. It should clearly specify which transaction sets will constitute a legally enforceable offer and acceptance and how electronic payments will be made. The parties should acknowledge that they will not repudiate the validity, integrity, or reliability of EDI transactions and will consider them the equivalent of paper-based transactions.

The parties must agree on the time and place of receipt of EDI communications. There are several possibilities. Receipt may take place when:

- A message is sent by the sender's computer system
- A message is received by the receiver's computer system
- A message is received at the receiver's mailbox on a VAN or other third party computer system
- An acknowledgement of receipt is sent by the recipient
- An acknowledgement of receipt is received by the sender.

Acknowledgements, typically used to verify communications, provide proof of a transaction's integrity and authority. Use cryptographic methods whenever possible, especially when the authenticity of a transaction is crucial. Sometimes electronic signatures are used to verify the integrity of a message; typically these signatures are created cryptographically. However, a signature doesn't have to be encrypted; any symbol or party's name may be considered sufficient as a signature for purposes of offer and acceptance as long as the EDI system is trustworthy. The location of the signature in messages should be agreed on in advance and be as uniform as possible.

Security considerations need special attention when you're drafting a trading partners agreement. Security provides confidence that transactions are authentic. It's needed to ensure that the transactions remain confidential. The EDI system's security is essential in determining whether electronic contracting is legally enforceable.

From a legal perspective trading partner agreements generally require *commercially reasonable security*—but the definition of commercially reasonable is vague, differing from industry to industry. For example, banking will require a much higher level of security than on-line retailing of software.

The trading partner agreement should discuss the security responsibilities of each party. For instance, to what extent is one party responsible for ensuring the security of its trading partner? What actions will be taken if security is breached? Basic EDI security risks include:

- Access violations
- Message modifications
- Interruptions or delays
- Message rerouting
- Message repudiation

Without access controls, an unauthorized individual could initiate a transaction by pretending to be an authorized trading partner. Fictitious purchase orders may be sent or fictitious payments made. The reliability and integrity of the EDI system break down without appropriate access controls. Greater security is achieved by combining several access control techniques. Most common are techniques based on:

- Something a person knows, such as a password
- Something a person possesses, such as a magnetic card or a token
- Some unique attribute of a person, such as a fingerprint, a voice print, or a retinal pattern

Unauthorized individuals may intentionally modify electronic messages. Messages may also be modified unintentionally through hardware, software, or transmission error. Authentication of messages is a major concern, especially with respect to repudiation of a transaction. Irrevocable proof, such as a digital signature, minimizes the risk of repudiation.

Auditing Contingency Plans

Data processing serves the information needs of most organizations and its survival in a disaster is often critical. Auditors are therefore especially concerned about the viability of the disaster recovery plan.

Your contingency plan is a valuable document that needs to be audited like any other asset. An auditor is responsible for investigating, evaluating, and verifying controls, which may reduce the risks associated with various types of disasters.

Avoiding disaster is always preferable to recovering from disaster. An effective contingency plan, audited regularly, can sometimes help prevent a disaster. For example, sabotage can be prevented, but when it isn't, saboteurs can often hide their activities. Auditing may help detect the crime.

Controls

Management is responsible for installing and maintaining controls, which are used to reduce the probability of attack on computer security. The auditor is responsible for determining whether the controls are adequate and whether they are being complied with. As more controls are incorporated, the operating costs tend to increase. Some types of controls are discussed below.

Deterrent controls are used to encourage compliance with controls. Deterrents are relatively inexpensive to implement. Since their purpose is to deter crime, however, it's often difficult to measure their effectiveness. Deterrent controls are meant to complement other controls; they're not sufficient by themselves.

Preventive controls are the first line of defense. Their purpose is to thwart perpetrators trying to gain access to your system. They also help prevent unintentional errors from affecting the system and the data. For example, pre-numbered documents ensure that there isn't a failure in recording a transaction. Data validation and review procedures prevent the recording of an incorrect or incomplete transaction, or duplicates of a transaction.

Detective controls help detect an error once a system has been violated. These controls prevent the error from harming the system. Their purpose is to focus attention on the problem. For example, a bait file will identify unauthorized use: A dummy (non-existent) record is processed. Or there may be a comparison between standard run time and actual run time to spot possible misuse.

Corrective controls reduce the impact of the threat after a loss has occurred. They aid in recovering from damage or in reducing the effect of damage. Corrective controls may provide data for recovery procedures. For instance, lost information on floppies may be restored with utility programs.

Application controls are built into software to deter or detect irregularities and minimize errors. Application controls typically include input, processing, change, testing, output, and procedural controls.

- *Input controls* are used to ensure that transactions are authorized, processed correctly, and processed only once. Input controls may reject, correct, or resubmit data.

- *Processing controls* ensure that transactions entered into the system are valid and accurate, that external data is not lost or altered, and that invalid transactions are reprocessed correctly.

- *Change controls* safeguard the integrity of the system. Standards are established for making modifications. All changes must be documented.

- *Test controls* ensure that a system is reliable before it becomes operational. An example would be the processing of limited test data when using the new system.

- *Output controls* authenticate other controls. They verify that authorized transactions are processed correctly. Random comparisons can be made of output to input to verify correct processing.

- *Procedural controls* help reduce the probability of processing mistakes and assure continued functioning if a failure does occur.

Audit Software

Computer-assisted audit techniques are used extensively; large quantities of electronically stored data can be tested quickly and accurately using audit software. Query languages can create ad hoc reports and perform a variety of audit procedures. Audit software functions typically:

- Appraise reasonableness (e.g., accuracy of sales discounts) and trends, including aging analysis
- Check for duplicate invoices or payments
- Compare financial data on different files for consistency

- Analyze and report data
- Extract data from computer files
- Provide exception reporting (e.g., excessive inventory balances or an unusual employee salary)
- Do field comparisons to find errors or inconsistencies
- Detect fraud
- Recalculate balances
- Do statistical sampling and analysis

Generalized audit software can identify errors keyed into accounting software. It provides cost savings over custom software because most audits involve similar activities, such as:

- Analyzing data for unusual or erroneous values
- Analyzing or comparing data stored in two or more separate but logically related files
- Generating and formatting reports
- Recalculating balances
- Selecting a sample
- Stratifying data
- Testing transactions

Examples of popular generalized audit software packages are ACL Software (888.669.4225 or *www.acl.com*) and Interactive Data Extraction and Analysis (IDEA) (888.641.2800 or *www.cica.ca*).

You can customize audit software if the generalized variety doesn't fulfill the needs of your organization. Specialized audit software is in any case available for specific industries, such as banking, health care, entertainment, or insurance.

Legal Liability in Security Management

Computer security law is a relatively new field, and the legal establishment has yet to reach a consensus on a host of important issues. Nonetheless, you can incur substantial legal liability by not maintaining adequate security. Management may be held personally liable in certain instances. Be particularly careful to protect privacy and other personal rights, which are easily violated due to a lack of computer security.

Legislation

The Financial Privacy Act of 1978 was passed to protect private information. The 1987 Computer Security Act further protects privacy and increases government computer security requirements. This act states that "improving the security and privacy of sensitive information in the federal computer systems is in the public interest." The private sector also has to ensure that confidential information is kept private.

The 1987 Computer Security Act gave the National Institute of Standards and Technology (NIST) responsibility to develop cost-effective standards to protect confidential information in federal databases. Private companies can use NIST's work as a model for their own standards.

Once information is determined to be sensitive, it should be verified for accuracy before being put into a database and given whatever protection is necessary to keep it confidential. Ask yourself the following questions:

- How should this information be classified?
- How can we ensure the accuracy of the information?
- How can we protect sensitive or confidential information?

The Computer Fraud and Abuse Act of 1986 makes any unauthorized use (copying, damaging, obtaining database information, etc.) of computer hardware or software across state lines a crime.

The Foreign Corrupt Practices Act of 1977 applies to companies whose securities are registered or filed under the Securities Exchange Act of 1934. It requires these companies to keep accurate accounting records and to maintain a system of internal control.

The Counterfeit Access Device and Computer Fraud and Abuse Act of 1984 covers unauthorized retrieval of data from the computer files of a financial institution or a credit reporting agency.

The Electronic Communications Privacy Act of 1986 prohibits anyone from intercepting information being transmitted electronically.

Negligence and Due Care

You can incur liability for security violations in a variety of situations, ranging from programming errors to violations of civil or criminal law. The standard to avoid liability is due care. For instance, you may have properly designed and coded a computer program but because security is inadequate, a saboteur places a logic bomb that causes the program to crash. The organization and its senior managers may be held personally liable for any damages arising from the crash if negligence in securing the program can be proved. Such damages may be significant if, for example, they cause a loss in market price of the stock or, worse, if human life is affected, as in the crash of a medical diagnosis system.

NIST has published several national standards for computer security. They cover:

- Automated password generators
- Contingency planning
- Data encryption
- Digital signatures
- Electrical power for computer facilities
- Key management
- Password usage
- Physical security and risk management
- User authentication techniques

The Department of Defense (DOD) publishes the Rainbow Series of booklets to help developers, evaluators, and users of trusted systems. They include information on networks, databases, and other problems with distributed computer systems. The governments of Britain, the Netherlands, France, and Germany have themselves jointly issued detailed Information Technology Security Evaluation Criteria (ITSEC).

Consider using these standards in managing your own computer security. If you don't, in a lawsuit alleging breach of security, the plaintiff may use your failure to follow recognized standards to prove that you've been negligent, even if your organization wasn't *required* to follow them.

Appendix
Security Software[1]

The following software may be used to improve the security of computers running on the Unix operating system. Several of these programs also have non-Unix versions.

Abacus Sentry detects the use of a port scanner in real time. Availability: *www.psionic.com/abacus/portsentry/*

Anonftpd is a read-only anonymous FTP server. Availability: anonymous ftp at *koobera.math.uic.edu*

Argus is a powerful tool for monitoring networks. It provides tools for analysis of network activity that can be used to verify the enforcement of network security policies, network performance analysis, and more. Availability: anonymous ftp at *ftp.sei.cmu.edu*

Arpwatch is an Ethernet monitor program that keeps track of Ethernet/IP address pairings. Availability: anonymous ftp at *ftp.ee.lbl.gov*

COPS (Computer Oracle and Password System) identifies security risks. It checks for empty passwords in /etc/passwrd, world-writable files, misconfigure anonymous ftp, and many others. Availability: anonymous ftp at *ftp.cert.org*

Courtney identifies the use of SATAN on a subnet. The program tcpdump (see below) will also be needed to run Courtney. Availability: anonymous ftp at *ciac.llnl.gov*

Crack is a password cracker. Availability: www at *www.users.dircon.co.uk*

---

[1] The material in this appendix was taken from *http://www.alw.nih.gov/Security/prog-full.html.*

Crack lib checks plain text words against those generated by Crack. Availability: anonymous ftp at *coast.cs.purdue.edu*

Deslogin provides a more secure method for remote log-in than Telnet or rlogin in untrusted networks. Deslogin encrypts the connection using DES. Availability: anonymous ftp at *ftp.uu.net*

Dig is a network utility that queries domain name servers; similar to nslookup but more flexible. Availability: anonymous ftp at *venera.isi.edu*

Drawbridge is a powerful bridging filter package. Availability: anonymous ftp at *net.tamu.edu*

Fping is an efficient way to test whether a large number of hosts are up. Availability: anonymous ftp at *slapshot.stanford.edu*

Icmpinfo displays unusual ICMP messages received by a host; it can be used to detect suspicious network activity. Availability: anonymous ftp at *hplyot.obspm.fr*

ISS checks hosts within a specified range of IP addresses for security vulnerabilities in send mail, anonymous FTP setup, NFS, and many more. Availability: anonymous ftp at *info.cert.org*

IPACL filters incoming and outgoing TCP and UDP in a SVR4/386 kernel. Availability: anonymous ftp at *ftp.win.tue.nl*

Kerberos is an authentication system used to protect unsecure networks (export restricted). Availability: WWW at *web.mit.edu*

Klaxon is a daemon used to identify the use of port scanners like ISS and SATAN. Availability: anonymous ftp at *ftp.eng.auburn.edu*

L6 provides a flexible and intelligent interface for periodic integrity checks of data using Perl. Availability: *www.pgci.ca/l6.html*

Logdaemon is a replacement for system ftp, rlogin, rexec, rshdaemons, and login program that has added security features, such as login in failures and S/Key one-time password support. Availability: anonymous ftp at *ftp.win.tue.nl*

Logsurfer analyzes any text-based log files on the fly, using contexts, and executes a corresponding action. Availability: anonymous ftp at *ftp.cert.dfn.de*

Lsof displays all open files on a Unix system. Availability: anonymous ftp at *vic.cc.purdue.edu*

Mangle is a utility that either checks existing passwords for weakness or forces users to choose good passwords. Availability: anonymous ftp at *ftp.informatik.uni-erlangen.de*

Merlin is an interface to five popular security packages to make it easier to analyze and manage the data. Availability: anonymous ftp at *ciac.llnl.gov*

MD5 is a hash function using the authenticity of the file. Availability: anonymous ftp at *rsa.com*

MIME Object Security Services (MOSS) is an extension of Multi-Purpose Internet Mail Extensions (MIME) that provides authentication, integrity, and confidentiality to an e-mail message (export restricted). Availability: anonymous ftp at *ftp.tis.com*

Netlog is network logging and monitoring of all TCP and UDP connections on a subnet; it includes tools to analyze the output. Availability: anonymous ftp at net.tamu.edu

Network Security Scanner (NSS) is a Perl that scans one host on subnet or an entire subnet for simple security problems. Availability: anonymous ftp at *jhunix.hcf.jhu.edu*

NFSWatch monitors NFS request and measures response time for each RPC. Availability: anonymous ftp at *coast.cs.purdue.edu*

Nmap (Network Mapper) is a utility for stealth port scanning of large networks (see Syn for tracking these types of scans). Availability: *www.insecure.org/nmap*

Npasswd is a replacement for the system passwd command that does not accept poor passwords. Availability: anonymous ftp at *ftp.cc.utexas.edu*

OPIE provides the ability to generate and use one-time passwords. (Related tools are also available for Windows, DOS, and Mac.) Availability: anonymous ftp at *ftp.nrl.navy.mil*

Osh is a restricted C shell that allows the administrator to control access to files and directories and to provide logging. Availability: anonymous ftp at *ftp.c3.lanl.gov*

Passwd+ is a proactive password checker that replaces the system passwd command and enforces the selection of good passwords. Availability: anonymous ftp at *ftp.dartmouth.edu*

PGP (Pretty Good Privacy) protects documents such as e-mail from unauthorized reading using public-key encryption (some versions are export-restricted). Availability: US and Canada: anonymous ftp at *www.eff.org* or via web form; international: anonymous ftp at *ftp.ifi.uio.no*

Pinglogger detects and logs ICMP echo requests. Availability: WWW at *www.students.uiuc.edu*

Portmapper reduces vulnerabilities and disallows proxy access. Availability: anonymous ftp at *ftp.win.tue.nl*

RIPEM (Riordan's Internet Privacy Enhanced Mail) improves the security of e-mail by verifying the authenticity of the message sender, among others things (export restricted). Availability: anonymous ftp at *ripem.msu.edu*

Rpcbind prevents intruders from bypassing NFS export restrictions. Availability: anonymous ftp at *ftp.win.tue.nl*

Rscan is an extensible network scanner that checks for common network problems and SGI-specific vulnerabilities. Availability: anonymous ftp at *ftp.vis.colostate.edu*

SATAN is a program that gathers information about the network, such as the type of machines, the services available on these machines, and potential security flaws. Availability: anonymous ftp at *ftp.win.tue.nl;* see also *wzv.win.tue.nl* for a list of mirror sites.

Scan-Detector determines when an automated scan of UDP/TCP ports is being done on a host running this program. Logs to either syslog or strerr. Availability: anonymous ftp at *coast.cs.purdue.edu*

Sendmail, a replacement for the system sendmail, this version includes all the latest patches. Availability: anonymous ftp at *ftp.cs.berkeley.edu*

Sendmail Wrapper provides limited protection against local sendmail attacks. Availability: anonymous ftp at *ftp.auscert.org.au*

Shadow includes everything necessary to use the shadow password file. Availability: anonymous ftp at *ftp.cs.widener.edu*

Simple Socksd is another implementation of Version 4 SOCKS protocol that is fast, easy to compile, and simple to configure. Availability: http at *Simple SOCKS Daemon*

SKey generates one-time passwords to gain authenticated access to computer hosts. Availability: anonymous ftp at *thumper.bellcore.com* or *coast.cs.purdue.edu*

SKIP (Simple Key-Management for Internet Protocols) adds privacy and authentication at the network level. Availability: US and Canada: via web form; international: anonymous ftp at *ftp.elvis.ru*

Smrsh is a restricted shell for sendmail to limit the number of programs that can be executed by sendmail. Availability: anonymous ftp at *ftp.nec.com*

Socks is a package that allows various Internet services, such as gopher, ftp, and Telnet, to be used through a firewall. Availability: anonymous ftp at *ftp.nec.com*

SSH (Secure Shell) is an advanced version of rlogin, rsh, and rcp that provides RSA authentication and encryption of communications as well as many other security improvements (export restricted). Availability: anonymous ftp at *ftp.cs.hut.fi*

STEL, a system replacement for Telnet, provides strong mutual authentication and encryption. Availability: anonymous ftp at *idea.sec.dsi.unimi.it*

Strobe displays all active listening TCP ports on remote hosts. It uses an algorithm that efficiently uses network band-width. Availability: anonymous ftp at *suburbia.apana.org* or *minnie.cs.adfa.oz.au*

Sudo allows a system administrator to give limited root privileges to users and logs their activities. This version is also known as CU-sudo. Availability: anonymous ftp at *ftp.cs.colorado.edu*

Swatch monitors and filters log files and executes a specified action, depending on the pattern in the log. Availability: anonymous ftp at *ee.stanford.edu*

Syn is a Perl utility for tracking steal port scanning. Availability: anonymous ftp at Syn *www.bigfat.net/unix.html*

TCP Wrapper allows a Unix system administrator to control access to network services; it also provides logging information of wrapped networks services that may be used to prevent or monitor network attacks. Availability: anonymous ftp at *ftp.win.tue.nl*

Tcpdump captures and dumps protocol packets to monitor or debug a network. Availability: anonymous ftp at *ftp.ee.lbl.gov*

Tcpr is a set of Perl scripts that forwards ftp and Telnet commands across a firewall. Availability: anonymous ftp at *ftp.alantec.com*

Tiger checks for known security vulnerabilities of Unix workstations; it's similar to COPS with many extensions. Availability: anonymous ftp at net.tamu.edu

TIS Firewall Toolkit is a software package to build and maintain a system to protect a network from unwanted activities. Availability: anonymous ftp at *ftp.tis.com*

Traceroute traces the route IP packets take from the current system to a destination system. Availability: anonymous ftp at *ftp.psc.edu*

Tripwire monitors for changes in system binaries. Availability: anonymous ftp at *coast.cs.purdue.edu*

TTY-Watcher monitors, logs, and interacts with all of the TTY on a system. Availability: anonymous ftp at *coast.cs.purdue.edu*

Wu-ftpd is a replacement FTP server for Unix systems whose features include extensive logging and a way of limiting the number of FTP users. Availability: anonymous ftp at *wuarchive.wustl.edu*

Xinetd is a replacement for inetd that has extensive logging and access control capabilities for both TCP and UDP services. Availability: anonymous ftp at *qiclab.scn.rain.com*

Xp-BETA is an application gateway for the X11 protocol that uses Socks or CERN WWW Proxy. Availability: anonymous ftp at *ftp.mri.co.jp*

YPX is a utility used to retrieve an NIS map from a host running the NIS daemon. Availability: anonymous ftp at *ftp.uu.net* or WWW server at *mls.saic.com*

Index

10T Base Unit, 27

A

Abacus Sentry, 235
Access, 20, 35. *See also* Calendar
  access; Electronic mail; Facilities;
  Files; Information; Logical
  access; Password-protected
  access; Physical access; Read
  access; Remote access; Write
  access.
  control card, 30
  denial, 117
  privileges, 176. *See also* Users.
  requirement, 21
  securing. *See* Network.
  sharing, 183
  termination, 183
Access control, 19-21, 47, 49, 101-
  102, 129. *See also* Granular access
  control.
  rules, 76
  system, 37
  usage. *See* Multiple users.
Access Control Module (ACM), 43
Accidental loss, 170
Account administration, 175-176
Account assignment, 175
Account ID, 175
Accounting departments, 194
ACM. *See* Access Control Module.

Action sequences, 209
Activation fees, 199
Active iris recognition system, 54
Active tests, 144
Active zone, 30
ActiveX, 72
  applets, 80
  code, 73
Activities, logging, 75
ADT, 38
AICPA, 225, 226
Air conditioning, 200
Alarm location, 209
Alarm reports. *See* Network-based
  alarm reports.
Analysis. *See* Business Impact
Analysis; Data; Risk.
  worksheet. *See* Business impact
  analysis worksheet.
Annoying event, 70
Anonftpd, 235
ANSI C source code, 136
Anti-harassment procedures, 186
Anti-static floor, usage, 16
Anti-static sprays, usage, 16
Anti-theft information, 28
Anti-virus programs, 71
Anti-virus scanning, 80
Anti-virus software, 63, 70-74, 93
Anti-virus solutions, 73
Appliance-like firewalls, 39